Published and Distributed by:

Granite Publishing and Distribution, LLC
868 North 1430 West
Orem, Utah 84057
(801) 229-9023 • Toll Free (800) 574-5779
Fax (801) 229-1924


Cover Design: Steve Gray
Page Layout and Design: Lyndell Lutes
Editing: Kenneth Lutes

ISBN 10: 1-59936-015-2
ISBN 13: 978-1-59936-015-7
Library of Congress Control Number: 2006940189

First Printing February 2007

10 9 8 7 6 5 4 3 2 1

PRINTED IN THE UNITED STATES OF AMERICA

Printed by FC Printing, Salt Lake City, UT

# The Triumphs of the Twelve

Holly Danneman

To my returned missionary sons,
Frederick and Mark,
who have also faithfully
carried the flame

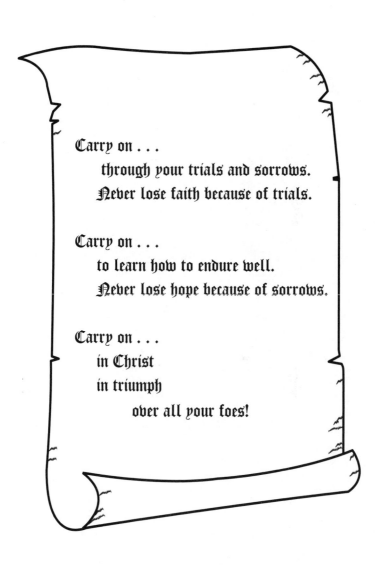

Carry on . . .
through your trials and sorrows.
Never lose faith because of trials.

Carry on . . .
to learn how to endure well.
Never lose hope because of sorrows.

Carry on . . .
in Christ
in triumph
over all your foes!

# Contents

# PREFACE

**I** write this book, focused mainly on the initial thirteen Apostles of our Lord and Savior Jesus Christ, as the first of my intended volume set devoted to the further study of them, our Savior, and His other followers. They lived in brutal times, and they all coped by working together for God.

The first thing readers will notice is that the order of the Apostles is arranged differently from other books. Here they are listed in order of their blood relationship to Jesus, which will be clarified soon. That is why Simon Peter is listed fourth, with Jesus' other cousins. The first three, listed in order of prominence, are blood brothers to Jesus through their mother, Mary, a claim I will make throughout this work. Usually, these three are placed at the end of lists, next to Judas Iscariot. They deserve better. (In addressing the problems of Jesus' family relationships, I was greatly helped by the book, *James, the Brother of Jesus* by Robert Eisenman.)

There are other sections of interest in this book that help us understand the events surrounding the thirteen Apostles. One chart lists all the women of the New

Testament. To give a historical view without getting bogged down in the narrative, I composed a detailed chronology from 48 B.C. to A.D. 70 that lists events and cultural tidbits.

Part of the joy of writing, for me, is that I am able to learn more about the subject than I could possibly have imagined. I had always questioned why the twelve faithful Apostles had to die so horribly. Yet, they faced their deaths, not with dread or fear, but with reverence to our Savior (Romans 8:16–18, 21; 1 Peter 4:12–14).

I learned in Hebrews 9:16–17 that their own laws dictated that they would earn martyrs' crowns, "For where a testament is, there must also of necessity be the death of the testator. For a testament is of force after men are dead: otherwise it is of no strength at all while the testator liveth."

Their love and reverence for their Master transformed their morbid fates into astoundingly inspiring triumphs of personal dignity. The Twelve (Matthias replacing Judas Iscariot) went willingly and joyfully to their decreed fates, begging God to forgive their murderers—and some converting their very accusers, and others. "History tells us the amazing fact that in spite of all the suffering Peter was subjected to, he converted his gaolers [jailers], Processus, Martinianus, and 47 others." [1]

In researching the lives of these thirteen men, I have also learned more about Jesus Christ and about the value of families. I really had no idea, when I first started, that Jesus had so many blood connections with His Apostles.

Yet, it makes sense. Just as the infant Jesus was "dependent" on His mother, Mary, and His stepfather, Joseph, to save Him from murderous King Herod, so also, as an adult, Jesus was "dependent" upon family, both men and women—to not undercut Him but rather to support Him during His public ministry and sacrifice. Indeed, many women relatives traveled with Him and the Apostles to minister to their needs. This family, with the Apostles and their families, rose to their challenges and collectively supported Jesus. What a triumph!

As is written periodically in our scriptures, the Bible does not contain a hundredth part of His works or His teachings. Nevertheless, for the less than a hundredth part we do have of Jesus Christ's condescension to show us how to act, we are indebted to these Twelve Apostles and their followers.

And it is enough to inspire us to triumph together, as they did, over all troubles . . . with faith in Christ . . . prayers to God . . . and love one for another, even as He loves us.

# ACKNOWLEDGMENTS

I would like to thank my assistant, Donna Vazquez, for all of her time spent researching and typing this book. There was tough competition vying for her talents from her patient husband and two adorable children. Therefore, additional thanks go to Donna's family for amiably sharing her with me.

I am also grateful and indebted to those who read drafts of the manuscript for their inspiration, support, and valuable input in shaping and refining this work.

The people who really made this book possible, however, are the valuable staff and resource people of Granite Publishing. Thank you for your guidance and encouragement—and for doing it all "first class"!

# Editorial Note

Most of this book is paraphrased and quoted from the *Parallel Bible of 1884* (referred to hereafter as the *PB*, see the introduction following). As well as being rare, the *PB* is a very large, hardback, leather-bound, five-inch-thick book with over two thousand pages, measuring nine by eleven-and-a-half inches. Extractions from the *PB* in this work have been condensed and edited where necessary to make them more reader-friendly for our day. We have tried to maintain the flavor of the nineteenth-century writers by using their words, except where it would be awkward or possibly cause misunderstanding. To avoid clutter, endnotes and quotation marks are used sparingly. Read this work with the idea of reading a very condensed version of selections from the *PB*.

In order to give the reader as much information as possible, dates, facts, and other items of interest from other sources have been included in the selected portions of the *PB* without necessarily indicating the particular source with an endnote. Most of the information has been consolidated from the five books listed in the introduction.

Please enjoy learning what these many different sources indicate about the original thirteen Apostles, without expecting extensive and precise endnotes as might be used in a scholarly discourse. Scholars should consider this an overview and should check the original sources for particulars—also, please note the detailed chronology at the end of this book that was compiled from the many works listed in the bibliography.

In summary, this work is intended to provide the best information the author has been able to obtain regarding these original thirteen Apostles, without encumbering the reader with laborious reference details.

# INTRODUCTION

**M**ost of the main reference sources for this book come from the pages of five books. Two of the books are Bibles, and the rest are also religious. One Bible is a modern King James Version, and the other is *The "Standard" Edition of The Holy Bible: Containing the King James and the Revised Versions of the Old and New Testaments Arranged in Parallel Columns,* commonly referred to as the *Parallel Bible of 1884.* More is explained about it on the following pages. The third book is the *Life of Christ* by John Fleetwood, D.D., and dates from 1866. The fourth main source is *Jesus the Christ* by James E. Talmage, and the fifth is *The Search for the Twelve Apostles* by William Steuart McBirnie.

In this work, these five books are coordinated with various other historical and apocryphal sources. This information is noted as it appears in the endnotes. The many ponderous, scholarly facts are edited into a more reader-friendly format for our time.

Many of the facts cited and the illustrations are from the *Parallel Bible of 1884.* An excerpt from its preface follows this introduction and explains how the work originated and the many sources of information used.

From this valuable *Parallel Bible*, edited biographies of each Apostle are presented. Also included are many facts from *The Search for the Twelve Apostles*. For some of the Apostles, commentaries are also included that were gleaned from the *Life of Christ* and *Jesus the Christ* about any New Testament text that is written by that particular Apostle. Since James the Just organized the first and chief Church, a list of interesting information about the Church in Jerusalem is included in his biography. For John's book of Revelation, in addition to the commentary, a chart is also included that simplifies and links the seven seals of the earth's events to their specific chapters and verses.

There is some disagreement about the birth of Christ—occurring anywhere from 7 B.C. to A.D. 1. James Talmage noted how difficult it was to get an accurate date.[2] For the sake of consistency, this work stayed with the *Parallel Bible* text that indicates He was born in 4 B.C. and crucified in A.D. 30. The rest of the dates for events are the ones most historians agree upon.

There is so much corroboratory material to support the Bible. After all, it is brimming with hints of many activities behind each scene that it narrates and each story that it tells. The backgrounds, cultural influences, and surrounding circumstances were not ever meant to be the focus; that is saved for the kings' historians to write in their own accounts. Rather, writers of the New Testament focused on testimonial accounts to inscribe.

Hence, the reason for its title "Testament."

In 2000 years of history, nothing has changed the truthfulness of New Testament principles, nor the earnestness of its many commentators. Both do remain a valuable resource for understanding the gospel better, for all ages, even this modern one. Historical and apocryphal writings add a richness of detail that enhance the verity of New Testament accounts.

All five of this book's main sources hint at or assert that Jesus had blood relatives among His Twelve Apostles. This work explains these relationships. Let us briefly explore various aspects surrounding this premise.

Having three of His younger half brothers (and possibly more) among His Apostles mixed in with four (and possibly six) of His cousins was problematic for all groups involved in our Savior's mortal ministry.

First and foremost, it was a problem for the Apostles themselves. More than once in their own accounts, we are told of situations where the Apostles debate among themselves as to whom the Lord loves the most. It is reasonable to assume that nonfamily members felt that preferential rewards would be given to family members over them. This was irrespective of Christ's repeated assurances that God loves all equally.

Second, it was a problem for the Jews on many levels. Having so many relatives supporting Jesus as He ministered was living proof that Jesus' words were truth indeed. It became especially important after His home village and synagogue rejected Him (Luke 4:16–30).

If Jesus was lying, none of His direct family members would be walking with Him and listening to Him. Such validation was critical after rejection from His village in a clime unencumbered with paper documents, identification cards, electronic records, and modern media scrutiny.

Coinciding with this is the Law of Witnesses, "In the mouth of two or three witnesses shall every word be established" (2 Corinthians 13:1). It states that two or three people are needed as witnesses to support any legal action against another. What better witnesses could Jesus have than to be able to produce from His close associates two or more people who knew Him from His childhood? The Pharisees and others simply could not refute so many witnesses—three half brothers and four cousins!

On the other hand, it also takes two or three witnesses to condemn anyone. Two disaffected family members or villagers could bring anyone down into condemnation. "At the mouth of two or three witnesses, shall he that is worthy of death be put to death; but at the mouth of one witness he shall not be put to death" (Deuteronomy 17:6).

Not one of Jesus' family witnessed against Him. What a *triumph* for His family! We can safely assume, given the relentless pursuit of the Pharisees and other Jewish leaders against Him, that they must have been promised bribes and otherwise pressured to witness against Jesus many times.

Your word was your bond.

Your works were your oath.

Your family was your literal life, or death.

To illustrate how critical the active support of family members was in those times, allow me to utilize a story from one of their own accounts. John 9 tells of Jesus giving sight to a man born blind. As this is the only account this author knows of where the full ramifications of Jesus' miracle are told, this story is worth studying and applying on many levels.

The shocked villagers take the healed man to the local Pharisees. An investigation is started. The man's parents are called in to testify and validate their son. In John 9:18–23, the parents verify that he is their son, but they refuse to support him—since he has received sight from Jesus—for fear of what their neighbors and the Pharisees might do.

They let go of their goodness. Horrible.

What happens to their son? Just as they have cast him out of their hearts and home, he is cast out of his village and denied the very means of his livelihood (John 9:34).

Who shows love to the outcast? Not his family, friends, neighbors, nor any villagers! Jesus does. In the very next verse, He searches him out to offer comfort and purpose to continue living his new life with sight.

This further explains why the Pharisees, Sadducees, and others could not dispute or stop Jesus' ministry until the appointed time of His Sacrifice. Jesus had the total support of His mortal family and the families of His Twelve Apostles.

Third, the problem for the Romans about what to do about Jesus' followers surfaced after His death and Resurrection. Josephus (A.D. 37–96) and many other historians wrote of how James, Judas, and Simon became vehemently anti-Roman, because it was the Romans who had carried out Jesus' Crucifixion.

After the Romans conquered and destroyed Jerusalem in A.D. 70, they made special efforts to seek out and kill all Jews who had any sympathy for Zealots, and with good reason. It was the Zealots, beginning with the Maccabeean (Hasmonean) family, who had caused contentions for centuries among both the Jews and Romans.

The conquered Jews had no qualms about relegating the three anti-Roman brothers to a lower status in their records, even so far as to label James as "the Less."

A fourth group who had problems with Jesus having brothers and cousins among the Twelve came centuries later in Rome when the religious movement of Catholicism grew into a church of its own. To justify their creed of celibacy for priests (which was *not* the practice of Jesus' Apostles), the Catholic writers further relegated the three brothers to having no blood connection at all—either to Jesus or to the Virgin Mary—and downplayed His cousins.

It is rare when such culturally and vowed enemies agree, but they did on this one false concept of Jesus having no blood relatives. But how to explain all of those ancient apocryphal and historical accounts and various scriptures that claim family ties? (see Matthew 13:55–56 and Galatians 1:19).

With this concept, a natural query arises that begs the question, *If Jesus had half brothers among the Apostles, then why did He assign John to care for His mother as He was dying, and not one of His own siblings?*

None of the other Apostles were there, for the simple reason that if they were there, they would have been taken and killed right then with Jesus. That is also why Peter so vehemently denied knowing Jesus three times during the previous night—to save his own life. He was being smart more than he was being a coward.

So, why was John, a cousin, allowed to be there and not be killed?

The answer is because of Mary, Jesus' mother. She had the right to be there. However, being old and grief-stricken, she was allowed to have a man with her to support her physically. It is reasonable that she chose John the Beloved over her own sons, sensing how much more painful it would be for them to see their good Brother suffer than it would be for John to witness it.

Jesus blessed their choice to be there together for Him by commissioning John to continue his support of Mary the rest of her life, thus honoring the Mosaic law concept of "an eye for an eye" by giving Mary "a son for a son."

Jesus so honored women with tender mercies, a rare concept for His day and culture.

# EXCERPT FROM THE PREFACE OF THE PARALLEL BIBLE

The present Revision had its origin in action taken by the Convocation of the Province of Canterbury in February, 1870. It has been conducted throughout on the plan laid down in Resolutions of both Houses of the Province.

Two Companies, the one for the revision of the Old Testament, and the other for the revision of the New Testament, were formed in the manner specified in the Resolutions. The work commenced on the twenty-second day of June, 1870.

Shortly afterwards, steps were taken under a resolution passed by both Houses of Convocation for inviting the co-operation of American scholars. Eventually two Committees were formed in America, for the purpose of acting with the two English Companies.

It was our privilege to have access to all of the original documents and scrolls to complete our work that was likewise used by the original translators who gave us the

King James Bible of 1611. Most of the documents were in Greek, their chief guides being the later editions of Stephanus, of Beza and the Complutensian Polyglott. Also available to our use were ancient Bible texts and Bibles from the very first, in various languages and forms.

Much illuminating information not restricted to Bible texts is no longer available to the public due to the advanced age of these many documents. So it is with pleasure that we also present collaborating facts, and copies of stunning illustrations to accompany the revised Bible text. Also, note that any scripture we quote in our chapters on the Bible texts are of our revised translation.

The whole time devoted to the work has been ten years and a half. The First Revision occupied about six years; the Second, about two years and a half. The remaining time has been spent in the consideration of the suggestions from America on the Second Revision, and of many details and reserved questions arising out of our own labors.

As a rule, a session of four days has been held every month (with the exception of August and September) in each year from the commencement of the work in June, 1870. The average attendance for the whole time has been sixteen each day. The whole Company consisted at first of twenty-seven scholars, but, for the greater part of the time of twenty-four members. Many of them reside at great distances from London. Of the original number, four have been removed from us by death.

# THE THIRTEEN APOSTLES

| Name of Apostle | Bible References | Relationship, Parents, Manner of death |
|---|---|---|
| James<br>  the Just<br>  the Younger<br>  the Less<br>  the Preacher | Matt. 10:3<br>Matt. 27:56<br>Mark 3:14–19<br>Mark 6:3<br>Mark 15:40<br>Luke 6:13–16<br>Acts 1:13<br>Gal. 1:19<br>Gal. 2:9<br>James 1:1 | • Brother of Jesus, Judas Lebbaeus and Simon the Zealot; son of Joseph and Escha or Mary; possibly son of Cleophas (Joseph's brother) or Alphaeus.<br>• Thrown off temple, stoned, then beaten to death with fuller's club in A.D. 62. |
| Judas Lebbaeus<br>Thaddeus (Jude) | Matt. 10:2–4<br>Matt. 13:55<br>Mark 3:14–19<br>Luke 6:13–16<br>Acts 1:13 | • Brother to Jesus, Simon the Zealot and James; son of Joseph and Mary; possibly son of Alphaeus or Cleophas.<br>• Martyred in Syria. Armenians say he died in Ardaze, Armenia A.D. 50. Another tradition says he lived to an old age. |
| Simon Zelotes<br>  the Zealot<br>  the Caananite | Matt. 10:2–4<br>Mark 3:14–19<br>Mark 15:40<br>Luke 6:13–16<br>John 19:25<br>Acts 1:13 | • Brother of Jesus, Judas Lebbaeus, and James; son of Joseph and Mary.<br>• One tradition says he was crucified in Britain, A.D. 44.<br>• Another says he was crucified by heretics in Rome at age 120. |

# The Triumphs of the Twelve

| Name of Apostle | Bible References | Relationship, Parents, Manner of death |
|---|---|---|
| Simon Peter<br>the Rock<br>Cephas | Matt. 10:2–4<br>Matt. 16:17<br>Mark 3:14–19<br>Luke 6:13–16<br>John 1:30–42<br>Acts 1:13 | • Cousin of Jesus; brother of Andrew; son of Jona (Jonas).<br>• Crucified head downward in Rome, A.D. 67, with wife and Paul.[3] |
| James<br>Boanerges<br>Son of Thunder<br>the Great | Matt. 10:2–4<br>Mark 3:14–19<br>Luke 6:13–16<br>Acts 1:13<br>Acts 12:2 | • Cousin of Jesus; brother of John Boanerges; son of Zebedee and Salome (Salome is Christ's mother's sister).<br>• Beheaded A.D. 44 in Jerusalem. |
| John<br>Boanerges<br>Son of Thunder<br>the Beloved<br>the Evangelist | Matt. 4:22<br>Matt. 10:2–4<br>Mark 3:14–19<br>Luke 6:13–16<br>John 21:20–23<br>Acts 1:13<br>Gal. 2:9 | • Cousin of Jesus; brother to James Boanerges; son of Zebedee and Salome.<br>• Tradition states he died in Ephesus in A.D. 95, but scriptures in John and D&C 7 state that he will remain alive until the Second Coming. |
| Andrew | Matt. 4:18<br>Matt. 10:2–4<br>Mark 3:14–19<br>Luke 6:13–16<br>John 1:30–42<br>Acts 1:13 | • Cousin to Jesus; brother to Simon Peter; son of Jona (Jonas).<br>• Crucified at Petra, on cross in form of letter X. Scourged; tied to cross to prolong death. Hung 2 days, preaching to people, died last day November, year unknown. |
| Philip | Matt. 10:3<br>Mark 3:14–19<br>Luke 6:14<br>John 1:43<br>Acts 1:13 | • Friend of Nathanael Bartholomew; parents not known.<br>• Died in Hierapolis in Phrygia, scourged, then crucified. |

# The Thirteen Apostles

| Name of Apostle | Bible References | Relationship, Parents, Manner of death |
|---|---|---|
| Nathanael Bartholomew | Matt 10:3<br>Mark 3:14–19<br>Luke 6:14<br>John 1:45–51<br>Acts 1:13 | • Friend of Philip; son of Talmai (Bartholomew meaning "son of Talmai").<br>• Was flayed alive and beheaded. Died at Albanopois in Armenia, A.D. 68. |
| Matthew Levi the Publican | Matt 10:3<br>Mark 2:14<br>Mark 3:14–19<br>Luke 6:14<br>Acts 1:13 | • Possibly the brother of Jesus, Judas, Simon, and James. Son of Alphaeus or Cleophas.<br>• One tradition indicates that he died a peaceful death; Acts of Andrew says he died in a fire at Anthropophagi. |
| Thomas Didymus "Doubting Thomas" | Matt. 10:3<br>Mark 3:14–19<br>Luke 6:14–15<br>John 11:16<br>John 14:5<br>Acts 1:13 | • Possibly Christ's younger brother, according to Nag Hammadi.<br>• Tradition indicates he was run through with a spear by the Brahmins near Meliapur, India. |
| Judas Iscariot the Traitor | Matt. 10:4<br>Matt. 27:3–5<br>Mark 3:14–19<br>Luke 6:14<br>John 6:71 | • No relation to any Apostle. From Judah. All others were Galilean.<br>• Son of Simon Iscariot.<br>• Committed suicide just prior to Christ's Crucifixion. |
| Matthias | Acts 1:23–26<br>1 Cor. 15:3–5<br>(Twelve mentioned as a group)<br>Rev. 21:14<br>(Twelve mentioned as a group) | • Called to apostleship out of pool of 120. No information on his family.<br>• Different traditions as to his death; may have died at Sebastopol; or stoned and beheaded by Jews; or crucified in Cappadocia between A.D. 61 and 64. |

# Bible Lists of the Twelve Apostles

**1. Matthew 10:2–4**

Now the names of the twelve apostles are these; The first, Simon, who is called Peter, and Andrew his brother; James the son of Zebedee, and John his brother;

Philip, and Bartholomew; Thomas, and Matthew the publican; James the son of Alphaeus, and Lebbaeus, whose surname was Thaddaeus;

Simon the Canaanite, and Judas Iscariot, who also betrayed him.

**2. Mark 3:14–19**

And he ordained twelve, that they should be with him, and that he might send them forth to preach,

And to have power to heal sicknesses, and to cast out devils:

And Simon he surnamed Peter;

And James the son of Zebedee, and John the brother of James; and he surnamed them Boanerges, which is, The sons of thunder:

And Andrew, and Philip, and Bartholomew, and Matthew, and Thomas, and James the son of Alpheus, and Thaddeus, and Simon the Canaanite,

And Judas Iscariot, which also betrayed him: and they went into a house.

### 3. Luke 6:14–16

Simon, (whom he also named Peter,) and Andrew his brother, James and John, Philip and Bartholomew,

Matthew and Thomas, James the son of Alphaeus, and Simon called Zelotes,

And Judas the brother of James, and Judas Iscariot, which also was the traitor.

### 4. John 1:35–47

Again the next day after John stood, and two of his disciples;

And looking upon Jesus as he walked, he saith, Behold the Lamb of God!

And the two disciples heard him speak, and they followed Jesus.

Then Jesus turned, and saw them following, and saith unto them, What seek ye? They said unto him, Rabbi, (which is to say, being interpreted, Master,) where dwellest thou?

He saith unto them, Come and see. They came and saw where he dwelt, and abode with him that day: for it was about the tenth hour.

One of the two which heard John speak, and followed him, was Andrew, Simon Peter's brother.

He first findeth his own brother Simon, and saith unto him, We have found the Messias, which is, being interpreted, the Christ.

And he brought him to Jesus. And when Jesus beheld him, he said, Thou art Simon the son of Jona: thou shalt be called Cephas, which is by interpretation, A stone.

The day following Jesus would go forth into Galilee, and findeth Philip, and saith unto him, Follow me.

Now Philip was of Bethsaida, the city of Andrew and Peter.

Philip findeth Nathanael, and saith unto him, We have found him, of whom Moses in the law, and the prophets, did write, Jesus of Nazareth, the son of Joseph.

And Nathanael said unto him, Can there any good thing come out of Nazareth? Philip saith unto him, Come and see.

Jesus saw Nathanael coming to him, and saith of him, Behold an Israelite indeed, in whom there is no guile!

## 5. Acts 1:13

And when they were come in, they went up into an upper room, where abode both Peter, and James, and John, and Andrew, Philip, and Thomas, Bartholomew, and Matthew, James the son of Alphaeus, and Simon Zelotes, and Judas the brother of James.

## 6. 1 Cor. 12:28–31 and Eph. 2:19–20; 4:11–14

Apostles in Church organization.

# CONFUSION OF APOSTOLIC NAMES

The number of instances among the men of the Apostolic Age of two persons bearing the same name is very curious. Among the Twelve, there are two Simons, two named James, and two named Judas. Including those whose labors were in any way connected with theirs, there are additionally two Johns (the Baptist and John Mark) and two Philips, besides other minor coincidences.

The confusion that this repetition of names causes among common readers is truly undesirable and it requires attention for them to avoid error.

Let us consider Judas. Matthew and Mark, in their lists of the Apostles, mention in the tenth place the name of Thaddaeus, also Lebbaeus. They give him a place before Simon Zelotes and after James. Luke gives the tenth place to Simon Zelotes in both his lists, and after him lists "Judas, the brother of James." John speaks of "Judas" (not Iscariot) among the chosen Apostles. Jude, in his own epistle, announces himself as "the brother of James," but omits mentioning Jesus.

From all these circumstances, it would seem that Judas or Jude (the brother of James) and Lebbaeus or Thaddaeus were all only different names of the same Apostle.

Furthermore, there is still another question connected with the simple existence and identity of Jude. Ancient traditions make mention of a Thaddeus, who first preached the gospel in the interior part of Syria. The question is whether he is the same person as the Apostle Jude, who is called Thaddeus by Matthew and Mark. The great majority of ancient writers, more especially the Syrians, consider the missionary Thaddeus not one of the Twelve Apostles, but rather one of the seventy disciples sent out by Jesus in the same way as the select Twelve.

However, this view is not universally received. Some scholars declare that these two sets of names referred to different persons, both of whom were at different times numbered among the Twelve Apostles. While others have also declared that names were added or excluded from the list by Jesus due to various circumstances, now unknown. One evangelist or another perhaps categorized some names according to the notions and individual preferences of each writer. Yet, others may have been nicknames.

Now consider another confusion of names that occurs with Alphaeus, Cleopas, and Cleophas. Alphaeus is listed as the father to James—who this writer contends is the Lord's blood brother (Matt. 10:3; Mark 3:18; Luke 6:15; Acts 1:13)—and Matthew Levi (Mark 2:14). Cleopas is a traveler with Simon (Luke 24:18–35) and Cleophas is the husband to Mary (John 19:25).

Some scholars think these three separately named men are one and the same man, namely Cleophas, the husband of Mary. Oddly, this particular Mary is never listed again.

Other scholars say that this Mary is the sister of Mary, the mother of Jesus (John 19:25). This makes James a cousin to Jesus, not a brother. However, it is extremely doubtful that parents would name two living daughters the same name, that of Mary. Mary's sister's name is actually Salome, who had at least two sons with her husband, Zebedee. This means that her two sons, James and John, were first cousins to Jesus.

To clarify the identities of the many women listed in the New Testament, there is a chart titled Women and the Work, further on in this work.

Confused? So are the scholars. There are many conflicting opinions one can read on this topic!

A little known name inconsistency is the name modern Christians use for our Savior. The Hebrew form of His name is *Yeshu'a* and means "the help of Yahveh." The English form of *Yeshu'a* is not "Jesus" but is actually "Joshua"! The Latin form of *Yeshu'a* is "Iesus." The Latin was probably anglicized to "Jesus" because it pronounces more closely to His Hebrew name.[4]

This author agrees with some historians that there was a concerted effort by the Jews, Romans, and later, Catholics, to conceal the actual blood relationships between Jesus and James (and hence Simon Zelotes and Judas). This is already explained in the introduction.

I also agree with the 27 biblical scholars—who compiled the *Parallel Bible* over a 14-year period and from which the apostolic biographies are taken—that James, Judas, and Simon Zelotes were blood brothers of Jesus Christ and that Peter, Andrew, James, and John were first cousins.

Note that all terms for "sister" and "brother" (Hebrew "ach" and "acoth" or Greek "adelphos" and "adelphe") can mean either from the womb, connected (near); or they may mean much like (remote)—that is, actual brother or sister; or cousin, aunt, uncle, son, niece, or nephew.[5]

*Hath not God chosen the poor of this world rich in faith, and heirs of the kingdom which he hath promised to them that love him?*

—James 2:5

The legacy of these
Twelve Apostles of Jesus Christ
is for all time and for all ages.
Each life, touched by Jesus Himself,
was empowered to become
more courageous, more fearless,
and more loving.

𐬺

These are their stories . . .

# James the Just

*If any of you lack wisdom, let him ask of God, that giveth to all men liberally, and upbraideth not; and it shall be given him. But let him ask in faith, nothing wavering.*

—James 1:5–6

# JAMES THE JUST

It has been doubted by some, whether James the Less was the same as that James who was afterwards bishop of Jerusalem—two men named James being mentioned in the sacred writings, namely, James the Great and James the Less, both Apostles.

The ancients also mentioned a third James, surnamed "the Just," whom they believed to be distinct from the former, and the bishop of Jerusalem. But this opinion is built upon a sandy foundation, for nothing is plainer than that James the Apostle—whom Paul calls our Lord's brother, and reckons with Simon Peter, and James and John Boanerges that he was one of the pillars of the Church—was the same who presided among the Apostles. This was doubtless by virtue of his episcopal office.

It is thought by some historians that he was the son of Joseph—afterwards the husband of Mary—by his first wife, Escha, the daughter of Aggi, brother to Zacharias, who was the father of John the Baptist. In any event, he was presumed to be our Lord's brother (Galatians 1:19).

We find, indeed, several men mentioned as the brethren of our Savior in the evangelical history, but in what sense was greatly argued by the ancients. Jerome (A.D. 347–420), Chrysostom (archbishop of Constantinople, lived A.D. 347–407), and some others, believed them to be called brothers because of their being the sons of Mary—cousin-german [first cousin], or, according to the Hebrew idiom, sister to the Virgin Mary (addressed in the previous section). But Eusebius (A.D. 263?–340), Epiphanius (patriarch of Constantinople A.D. 520–535), and many others, tell us they were the children of Joseph by a former wife, Escha. James Talmage noted the difficulty of sorting conflicting facts out as well.[6]

However, Gamaliel (Acts 5:34; 22:3) was sent by the Jewish Sanhedrin[7] to investigate the validity of Jesus. During his interview with Joseph and Mary, he reports, rather harshly, that "their children (referring to those he saw younger than Jesus) look very much like him (Joseph), and upon the whole I should call them a third rate family."[8]

After the resurrection, James, as well as Peter, was honored with a particular appearance of our Lord to him, which, though passed over in silence by the evangelists, is recorded by Paul. Afterwards, Jesus appeared to His other Apostles. Some time after this appearance, James was chosen bishop of Jerusalem, to form the first Christian Church with 3,120 members. He was preferred before all the rest for his near relation to Christ, as dictated by following the patriarchal order to carry on the family legacy.

For the same reason, we find Simon Peter chosen to

be his immediate successor, because, after James, he also resided in Jerusalem and was also kinsman to our Lord. Though our Savior had particularly honored them, such a consideration made Peter and the two sons of Zebedee, not to contend for this high and honorable station, but to freely choose James the Just bishop of Jerusalem.

James, as head of the first Christian Church, held the keys of the ministry and priesthood power until his martyrdom in A.D. 62. Peter (who traditionally became the second head of "Christendom"), James (who was beheaded earlier in A.D. 44), and John also held them.

"And I will make thee to minister for him and for thy brother James; and unto you three I will give this power and the keys of this ministry until I come" (D&C 7:7).

It was to James that Peter sent the news of his miraculous deliverance out of prison (Acts 12:17): "Go," said he, "shew these things unto James, and unto the brethren;" that is, to the whole Church, especially to James, the pastor of it.

James performed every part of his duty with all possible care and industry. He strengthened the weak, instructed the ignorant, reduced the erroneous, and reproved the obstinate. Thus, by the constancy of his sermons, he conquered the stubbornness of that perverse generation he had to deal with. Many of the nobler and richer sort were persuaded to embrace this new Christian faith. In fact, so great was the prominence of James in Jerusalem that there are many writings by historians that greatly enlarge what little is found in our current canon.

A person so careful, so successful in his charge, could not fail to excite the spite and malice of his enemies. They were the sort of men of whom the Apostle had given too true a character, that they "please not God, and are contrary to all men." They were vexed to see Paul escape their hands by appealing unto Caesar and therefore turned their fury against James.

Being unable to effect their design under the government of Festus, they determined to attempt it under the procuratorship of Albinus, his successor. Ananus the Younger, of the sect of the Sadducees, was high priest.

A council was summoned, and the Apostle, with others, was arraigned and condemned as violators of the law. So the action might appear more plausible and popular, the scribes and Pharisees—masters in the art of dissimulation—endeavored to ensnare him.

At their first coming, they told James that they had all placed the greatest confidence in him. The whole nation, as well as they, gave him the title of a just man and one who was no respecter of persons.

They therefore desired James to correct the error and false opinions the people had conceived of Jesus, whom they considered the Messiah—"Take this opportunity to set them right in their opinions in this particular." They urged that he go with them to the top of the temple where he might be seen and heard by all.

The Apostle readily consented. Being advantageously placed on a pinnacle of the temple, they addressed him in the following manner; "Tell us, for we have all the reason in the world to believe, that the people are generally led away with the doctrine of Jesus, who was crucified. Tell us, what is this institution of the crucified Jesus?"

To which James answered, with an audible voice, "Why do you inquire of Jesus, the Son of Man? He sits in heaven, at the right hand of the Majesty on High, and will come again in the clouds of heaven."

The people below hearing this, glorified Jesus, and openly proclaimed, "Hosanna to the Son of David!"

The scribes and Pharisees now perceived that they had acted foolishly; instead of altering the people in their belief, they had confirmed it. There was no way left but to destroy James immediately in order to warn others, by his sufferings, not to believe in Jesus of Nazareth. Accordingly, they suddenly cried out that James himself was seduced and had become an imposter.

They immediately threw him from the temple pinnacle on which he stood into the court below. But not being killed on the spot, he recovered himself so far as to rise on his knees and pray fervently to heaven for his murderers.

Malice is too diabolical to be pacified with kindness or satisfied with cruelty. Accordingly, his enemies, vexed that they had not fully accomplished their work, poured a shower of stones upon him while he was imploring their forgiveness at the throne of grace. One of them, dissatisfied with this cruel treatment, put an end to his misery by beating him with a fuller's club.

Josephus (A.D. 37–96), a Pharisee upon whose vivid

account we continue this narrative, obtained his information by interrogating prisoners.[9] So amazing was his memory that he was noticed by the Roman overseers and was elevated, while still a young man, to become an aide to Titus (A.D. 39–81), son of the Roman Emperor, Vespasian (A.D. 9–79, ruled A.D. 69–79). Such elevation of a Jew necessitated that he be adopted into the Roman imperial family.

This access allowed Josephus the leisure and materials to write out over many years his vast knowledge of his Jewish country folk, as well as write flatteries of his Roman benefactors.

It was with boldness that Josephus finished his narrative of the martyrdom of James with a prophetic judgment against his countrymen in Jerusalem. He wrote that the fall of Jerusalem in A.D. 70 was directly attributed to the Jews murdering James eight years earlier, as well as his brother, Jesus, decades before.

What influenced Josephus to make such a harrowing connection of these two martyrdoms to the destruction of his beloved city? In their own canon is found the Law of Witnesses:

"At the mouth of two witnesses, or three witnesses, shall he that is worthy of death be put to death; but at the mouth of one witness he shall not be put to death" (Deuteronomy 17:6).

When the Jewish populace actively rejected Jesus and sought His life, He was only one witness to Heavenly Father against their "children and their children's children" of His innocent martyrdom. But when His brother, James, was also martyred, he became a second witness to Heavenly Father against their "children and their children's children."

For God will not be mocked.

# Commentary on the Epistle of James

The ancient world was full of preachers. Dressed in a rough cloak, one would take his stand at some street corner to amuse and instruct, with his easy, animated talk, the chance crowd that gathered about him. He would mingle question and answer, apostrophe and dialogue, invective and anecdote. He would urge his little congregation to fortitude and self-control, the great ideals of the Stoic teachers. These street preachers of ancient times were Stoics and their sermons were called "diatribes."

Christian preachers had to compete with these men for the attention of the people they were trying to convert to Christianity. They naturally adopted some of their methods. In the marketplace at Athens, Paul did this informal open-air preaching every day. In so doing he came into conflict with some of these Stoic preachers. A later Stoic, Justin (Christian apologist, lived A.D. 100–165), became a Christian. He tells us in his *Dialogue with Trypho* how he continued to practice this way of preaching on the promenade at Ephesus (west Asia Minor).

We cannot help wishing that one of these street sermons had been preserved for us just as its author gave it. We have, in the book of Acts, reports of several sermons of Stephen, Peter, and Paul. Thankfully, we do have at least one ancient sermon preserved for its own sake and not as an incidental part of a historical narrative. We know the sermon as the Epistle of James.

In James, the Christian[10] preacher tells his hearers that life's trials, vicissitudes, and temptations will perfect character if they are met in dependence upon God. From this sermon we learn:

- His hearers must not merely profess religion but really practice purity and humanity.
- They must be doers that work, not hearers that forget.
- They must learn to respect the poor, to feed and clothe the needy.
- Their faith must show itself in good works.
- They must not be too eager to teach and direct one another.
- The tongue is the hardest thing in the world to tame.
- If they wish to show their wisdom, let them do it by a life of good works.
- They must give up their greed, indulgence, and worldliness, their censoriousness and self-confidence.
- Their rich oppressors are doomed to punishment, only they must be patient, like Job and the prophets.

- Above all, they must refrain from oaths.
- In trouble and sickness they must pray for one another.
- The prayer of a righteous man avails much.
- They must seek to convert sinners, for God especially blesses such work.

These are the teachings of this ancient sermon. What is the connection between them? Do they constitute a chain of thought? As an example of Christian preaching, this sermon is not at all doctrinal or intellectual. Little is said even of Christ. The whole emphasis is practical.

The preacher's interest is in the conduct—in the words and acts—of his hearers. He does not care especially about their theological views. For him the only real faith is that which shows itself in good deeds.

Honest, upright, and helpful living is what the preacher demands. He does so with directness and a frankness rarely surpassed. This has given this fifteen-minute sermon its abiding place in Christian literature.

Where this sermon was first preached is impossible to say. It would have been appropriate almost anywhere. That is the beauty of it. It contains none of those unmistakable epistolary touches that we find, for example, in Galatians and Second and Third John. It does not end with a farewell or benediction as so many New Testament letters do. Only the salutation contained in the first verse suggests a letter: "James, a servant of God and of the Lord Jesus Christ, to the Twelve Tribes which are scattered abroad, greeting."

However, a moment's reflection will show that this does not prove the Epistle of James to be a letter. How would one go about delivering it "to the Twelve Tribes which are scattered abroad," that is, to the Jews scattered about through the Greco-Roman world from Babylon to Spain? Or, if the Dispersion is meant in a figurative sense, to all the Christians outside Palestine?

It is clear at once that these words are not the salutation of a letter but a kind of dedication for a published work.

Like thousands of other sermons, it was not only preached but also published, with a dedication, boldly figurative, to Christians everywhere.

There is something very modern about this Epistle of James. Its interest in democracy, philanthropy, and social justice strikes a responsive chord in our time. The preacher's simplicity and directness, his impatience with whining and pretension shows his satirical skill in exposing them. His noble advocacy of the rights of labor and his clear perception of the sterling Christian virtues justify the place of honor his sermon has in the New Testament.

# The Church in Jerusalem[11]

1. Began at Pentecost with at least 3120 members and was pastored by James, the brother of Christ (Acts 2:47, 41; 15:13).
2. Preached the Word (Acts 2:16–36; 3:13–26; 7:1–53; 6:4; 5:42).

3. Practiced baptism and the Lord's Supper (Acts 2:41, 46).

4. Spent a good deal of time in prayer (Acts 2:42; 3:1; 4:24; 12:5–17).

5. Performed many wonders and signs (Acts 2:43; 5:12–16).

6. Believers had all things in common (Acts 2:44–45; 4:32–35).

7. Believers were in one accord (Acts 2:46).

8. Had Spirit-led believers (Acts 2:1–18; 4:31; 13:2–4; 15:28).

9. Grew constantly (Acts 2:47; 4:4; 5:14; 12:24).

10. Witnessed at every opportunity (Acts 3:12; 4:33; 5:42 ).

11. Endured persecution (Acts 4:1–3; 4:14–21; 5:17–41; 7:54–60; 8:1–3; 12:1–4).

12. Radiated Jesus (Acts 4:13; 6:15).

13. Was kept pure by God (Acts 5:1–11; 8:18–24).

14. Appointed deacons (Acts 6:1–7).

15. Sent forth missionaries (Acts 8:15; 11:22; 13:1–3; 14; 15:22, 27).

16. Contended for the faith (Acts 15:1–21).

17. Was the site of the important meeting on circumcision (Acts 15).

18. Apparently later compromised with the Judaizers (Acts 21:18–25).

# Judas Lebbaeus Thaddaeus (Jude)

*Keep yourselves in the love of God, looking for the mercy of our Lord Jesus Christ unto eternal life.*

—Jude 1:21

# JUDAS LEBBAEUS THADDAEUS (JUDE)

꧁꧂

Concerning this Apostle, is he the same as that Judas who is mentioned along with James, Joses, and Simon, as the brother of Jesus? (Galatians 1:19) All the important points involved in this question, have been already discussed in the life of James the Just. If the conclusion of that argument is correct, the irresistible consequence is that the Apostle Judas was also one of these brothers of Jesus (see Matthew 13:55).

The absurdity of the view of his being a different person cannot be better exposed than by a simple statement of its assertions. It requires the reader to believe that there was a Judas, a James, and a Simon, brothers and Apostles. Then there was another Judas, another James, and another Simon, also brothers, and brothers of Jesus, but not apostles. Third, that these are all mentioned in the New Testament without anything like a satisfactory explanation of the reality and distinctness of this remarkable duplication of brotherhoods.

Add to this, moreover, the circumstance that Judas specifies himself as "the brother of James," as though that were sufficient to prevent his being confounded with any other Judas or Jude in the world. This specification would be totally useless if there was another Judas, the brother of another James, all eminent Christian leaders. However, there was not.

So perfectly destitute are the gospel and apostolic history of the slightest account of this Apostle's life and actions, that the only word that has been preserved as coming from his lips to Jesus is recorded in John's account of the parting discourses of Jesus to His Apostles on the eve of His Crucifixion.

Jesus was promising them that the love of God should be the sign and the reward of him who faithfully kept His commandments—"He that hath my commandments, and keepeth them, he it is that loveth me: and he that loveth me shall be loved of my Father, and I will love him, and will manifest myself to him" (John 14:21).

These words constituted the occasion of the remark of Judas, thus recorded by John.

"Judas saith unto him, not Iscariot, Lord, how is it that thou wilt manifest thyself unto us, and not unto the world?

"Jesus answered and said unto him, If a man love me, he will keep my words: and my Father will love him, and we will come unto him, and make our abode with him" (John 14:22–23).

A natural inquiry, aptly and happily suggested, was

most clearly and satisfactorily answered in the plain but illustrative words of the Divine Teacher! Would that the trying efforts of all critical thought might end in results so brilliant and cheering!

The labors of Jude appear to have been confined chiefly to his own country. When he began his great message of mercy, he went up and down Judea and Galilee, and afterwards through Samaria into Idumea, and to the cities of Arabia, and the neighboring districts; after which he visited Syria and Mesopotamia. The success of his ministry is not particularly stated; but we have reason to know, that the ministry of our Apostle was no less successful in these parts, than that of his fellow Apostles in others.

He is believed also, on the almost general consent of the writers of the Latin Church, to have traveled into Persia. At first, he met with great opposition, yet ultimately, his apostolical ministry became eminently useful in turning many of the people from their superstitious rites to the truth of the gospel. Some early writers have even asserted that in this country he was cruelly put to death.

By Nicephorous (A.D. 758?–829), we are informed that Jude went to Edessa where Abgarus—a leper who was cured by Jude, and an apocryphal correspondent with the Savior (the "Abgarus Letters")—was governor. Here he met with a fellow laborer of his own name, and one of the Seventy. This latter individual had been sent to Abgarus, the governor, where, by healing diseases, working miracles, and expounding the doctrines of Christianity, the people had generally renounced their pagan worship, even prior to the reception of the blessed Jude amongst them.

In common with most of the Apostles, Jude was a married man. No particular account of his family indeed exists, excepting a singular incident concerning two of his grandsons. Eusebius (A.D. 260?–340?), on the authority of Hegesippus (died A.D.180), gives the following account:

> Domitian [A.D. 51–96], the emperor, whose enormous wickedness had awakened in him the quickest jealousies, making him suspect every one that might look like a co-rival in the empire, had heard that there were some of the line of David and Christ's kindred that did yet remain.
>
> Two grandchildren of Jude, the brother of our Lord, were brought before him. And having confessed that they were of the race and posterity of David, they were asked what possessions and estates they had. They told him that they had a very few acres of land, out of the improvement whereof they both paid tribute and maintained themselves with their own labor . . . .
>
> He then inquired of these concerning Christ, and the state of His kingdom—what kind of empire it was, and when, and where it would commence. To which they replied that His kingdom was not of this world, or of the . . . dominions of it, but heavenly and angelic; and which would finally be set up at the end of the world, when coming with great glory, Christ would judge the quick, and the dead, and reward or punish all men according to their works . . . .

## Judas Lebbaeus Thaddaeus (Jude)

Looking upon the weakness and simplicity of the men as below his jealousies and fears, he [Domitian] dismissed them without using any severity against them; and . . . these two, being now beheld not only as kinsmen, but as martyrs of our Lord, were honored by all, were preferred to places of authority and government in the Church, and lived till the time of Trajan [A.D. 52 or 53–117].

Soon after the time of Eusebius, seven catholic or general epistles were received by all Christians, Greeks, and Latins. Jude's Epistle was received by Athanasius, Cyril of Jerusalem, Epiphanius, Jerome, Rufin, Augustin, and others. This epistle was in the hands of many people, or of all Christians in general, to be consulted by them. Origen (A.D. 230) also has several plain quotations from Jude's Epistle.

The solitary monument and testimony of Jude's apostolic labors are found in that brief, but strongly characterized and peculiar writing which bears his name. Short as it is, and obscure too, by the numerous references it contains to local and temporary circumstances, there is much expressed in this little portion of the apostolic writings which is highly interesting to the inquirer into the darker portions of the earliest Christian history.

Several very remarkable circumstances in this epistle have, from the earliest ages of Christian theology, excited great inquiry among writers. In many cases, commentators and critics have pronounced the work very suspicious in its character, to even condemn it as unworthy of a place in the sacred canon.

One of these circumstances is that the writer quotes apocryphal books of a mystical and superstitious character that have never been received by Christians or Jews as possessing any divine authority nor as entitled to any regard whatever in religious matters.

At least two distinct quotations from these contested writings are found in this brief epistle of Jude (verses 14–16). One is from the book of Enoch, which has been preserved even to the present day (1884), in the Ethiopic translation, the original Hebrew having been irrecoverably lost.

Some of the highest authorities in orthodoxy and in learning have pronounced the original to have been a very ancient writing—a forgery indeed, since it professed to be the writing of Enoch himself but made up in the earliest ages of Rabbinical literature. After the Old Testament canon was completed, but before any portion of the New Testament was written, it dates some years before the Christian Era.

Another quotation, equally remarkable, occurs in this epistle of Jude (verses 5–11), without any mention having been made, however, of the exact source from which the passage has been drawn; and the point is at present a subject of dispute. Different authorities have referred, ancient and modern, to different apocryphal Jewish books, which contain similar messages.

The most valuable authorities decided it was a work now universally allowed to be apocryphal—the *Ascension* or *Assumption of Moses*—which is directly quoted as authority on a subject altogether removed from human knowledge. No testimony of it could be of any value except it were derived directly and solely from the sources of inspiration.

The whole defense of the epistle against these imputations may be grounded upon the supposition that the Apostle was writing against a peculiar class of heretics, called Gnostics, who did acknowledge these apocryphal books to be of divine authority. He might quote these with a view to show that even by their own standards of truth, their errors of doctrine and life must be condemned.

The sect of the Gnostics is the first ever known to have perverted the purity of Christian doctrine by heresy. These heretics certainly are not fully described in those few passages that are directed at the errors of doctrine. Nevertheless, the character of those errors, which Jude denounces, is accordant with what is known of some of the prominent peculiarities of the Gnostics.

The evils that he denounced, however, were not merely of a speculative character. He more especially condemns their gross immoralities as a scandal and an outrage on the purity of the Christian assemblies with which they still associated.

In all passages where these vices are referred to, it will be observed that both immoralities and doctrinal errors are included in one common condemnation. This shows that both were inseparably connected in the conduct of these heretics whom the writer condemns.

This circumstance also does much to identify them with some of the Gnostical sects alluded to before—more especially with the Nicolaitans, as they are called by John in the beginning of the Apocalypse where he is addressing the Church of Pergamos (modern-day Bergama in Turkey). With respect to this very remarkable peculiarity of a vicious and abominable life, combined with speculative errors, the ancient Christian writers fully describe the Nicolaitans. Their accounts are so unanimous and their accusations so definite, that it is just and reasonable to consider this epistle as directed particularly against them.

Another circumstance in this epistle that has attracted a critical notice is the remarkable coincidence both of sense and words between it and the second chapter of the Second Epistle of Peter.

There is no more reason to reject either of these texts based on their similarities than there is to reject any of the Gospels, for don't they all tell the same story but with various views?

Both of the Apostles were evidently denouncing the same errors and condemning the same vices. Nothing was more natural than that this similarity of purpose should produce a proportional similarity of language. Peter may have written first and Jude may have taken a portion of that epistle as furnishing hints for a more protracted view of these particular points. Or, on the supposition that Jude wrote first, Peter may have thought it worthwhile only to refer generally and not to dwell very particularly on those points which his fellow Apostle had already so powerfully treated.

The particular churches to which this epistle was addressed are unknown. Asia Minor, Syria, and the East were the regions to which the Gnostical errors were mostly confined. In the former country, more especially, they were objects of attention to the ministers of truth during the Apostolic Age and in succeeding times. It was probably intended for the same persons to whom Peter wrote. What has been said on the direction of his two epistles will illustrate the immediate design of this also.

Its date is involved in the same uncertainty that covers all points in its own history and that of its author, the prominent difficulty being its great brevity. It offers but few characteristics of any kind for the decision about doubtful points. The life and works of Judas must therefore be set down among those matters in which the indifference of the writer has left modern criticism not one hook to hang a guess upon.

The events surrounding the death of Judas are shrouded in legends and mysteries. The most persistent legend is from the Armenians, who assert that Judas died in Ardaze, Armenia in A.D. 50. However, others assert that he lived to a ripe old age.

# Commentary on the Epistle of Jude

Many ancient thinkers conceived of the supreme God as far removed from the material world and too pure to have anything directly to do with it. The necessary connection between God and the world, they thought, was made through a series of intermediate ideas, influences, or beings, to one of which they ascribed the creation and supervision of the material world.

When people with these views became Christians, they brought most of their philosophical ideas with them into the Church, and then combined them as far as they could with their new Christian faith.

In this way, there came to be many Christians who held that the God of this world could not be the Supreme God whom Jesus called His Father. Their view of Jesus Himself seemed to most Christians a denial of a Heavenly Father, for they held to the Docetic idea that the Divine Spirit left Him before His death.

They, accordingly, saw little religious meaning in His death, for they considered themselves so spiritual that they did not feel the need of an atonement. In fact, they felt so secure in their spirituality that they thought it did not much matter what they did in the flesh. Therefore, they permitted themselves all sorts of indulgences without scruple.

Such people could not help being a scandal in the churches, and a Christian teacher named Jude made them the object of a letter of unsparing condemnation.

## Judas Lebbaeus Thaddaeus (Jude)

He immediately sent his friends a short vehement letter condemning the immoral practices of these people, predicting their destruction and warning his readers against their influence.

He quotes against them, with the greatest confidence, passages from the book of Enoch and the *Ascension* or *Assumption of Moses*, late Jewish writings that he seems to regard as scripture. Jude looks back upon the age of these ancient prophets, asking his readers to recollect how they have foretold that as time draws on toward the end, scoffers will appear.

The persons he attacks still belong to Christian churches and attend Christian meetings. He does not tell his readers to exclude them from their fellowship but to have pity on them and try to save them, only taking care not to become infected with their faults.

# Simon Zelotes

*But these speak evil of those things which they know not:
but what they know naturally, as brute beasts, in those things
they corrupt themselves.*
—Jude 1:10

# SIMON ZELOTES

hird in family prominence to our Savior would surely be this third blood brother among His Apostles, Simon Zelotes. Simon is also styled Simon the Canaanite, whence there is some conjecture he was born in Cana of Galilee.

The word "Cana" is not related to his country, or the place of his nativity. It is derived from the Hebrew word *kana,* which signifies zeal, and denotes a warm and sprightly temper. What some of the evangelists call "Canaanite," others, rendering the Hebrew by the Greek work, call him "Zealot."

This is not so much from his great zeal, his ardent affection to his Master, and his desire of advancing his relation in the world, as it is from his warm, active temper and zealous forwardness in a particular sect before his joining with the Savior.

In order to understand this better, it will be necessary to observe that there was a distinct sect, or at least a branch of the Pharisees, called Zealots. This sect of the Zealots took upon themselves to execute punishments in extraordinary cases, with the permission both of the rulers and the people. In the process of time, their zeal degenerated into all kinds of immorality and wild extravagance. They not only became the pests of the commonwealth at home, but also opened the door for the Romans to break in upon them and the Jewish populace to their final and irrevocable ruin.

They were continually prompting the people to throw off the Roman yoke and assert their natural liberty. When they had thrown all these things into confusion, they took care to take advantage of the tumult. Josephus gives a large account of them and everywhere bewails them as the great plague of the nation.

Many attempts were made, especially by Annas, the high priest, to reduce them to order and oblige them to observe the rules of sobriety, but all were in vain. They continued their violent proceedings and, joining with the Idumeans (descendents of Esau, the Edomites), committed every kind of outrage. They broke into the sanctuary, slew the priests themselves before the altar, and filled the streets of Jerusalem with tumults, plunder, and blood.

Nay, when Jerusalem was closely besieged by the Roman army at various times, the Zealots continued their detestable proceedings. They created fresh tumults and factions, and were indeed the principal cause of the merciless slaughter and dispersion of the Jews in the fatal war of A.D. 70.

Whatever Simon was before, we have no reason to suspect but that after his conversion he was very zealous for the honor of his Master. He considered all those who were enemies to Christ as enemies to himself, however near they might be to Him in any natural relation.

He was very exact in all the practical duties of the Christian religion, so he showed a very serious and pious indignation towards those who professed religion and a faith in Christ with their mouths, but dishonored their sacred profession by their irregular and vicious lives. Some of the first professing Christians really did lead double lives.

Simon continued in communion with the rest of the Apostles and disciples at Jerusalem. At the Feast of the Pentecost he also received the same miraculous gifts of the Holy Ghost so that he was qualified, with the rest of the brethren, for the apostolic office. In propagating the gospel of the Son of God, we cannot doubt of his exercising his gifts with the same zeal and fidelity. His companion was sometimes his brother, Judas. He went into Egypt, Cyrene (Libya), Africa, and Mauretania (a province of northwest Africa), preaching the gospel to the inhabitants of those remote and barbarous countries.

Eusebius (bishop of Caesarea, lived A.D. 260?–340?) adds that after Simon had passed through those burning wastes, he took ship and visited the frozen regions of the north. He preached the gospel to the inhabitants of the western parts, even in Britain.

There, having converted great multitudes and sustained the greatest hardships and persecutions, he was at last crucified in Britain, probably in the east part in Caistor (Norfolk, UK) as it was under the prefecture of Caius

Decius. This Roman officer's atrocities were also the immediate cause of the Boadicean war of A.D. 60–61. Where Simon is buried is unknown.

# Simon Peter

*Thou art the Christ, the Son of the living God. And Jesus answered and said unto him, Blessed art thou, Simon Barjona: for flesh and blood hath not revealed [it] unto thee, but my Father which is in heaven.*

—Matthew 16:16–17

# SIMON PETER

**S**imon Peter, who appears most predominately at the head of most apostolic lists, comes before us abruptly. Two youths were following Jesus Christ, one of whom was Andrew, Simon's brother. He did not conceal the joyful discovery he had made; for early in the morning he hastened to acquaint his brother Simon that he had found the Messiah.

Simon, who was one of those who waited for redemption in Israel, ravished with this joyful news, and, impatient of delay, followed his brother to the place. On his arrival, our Savior immediately gave him a proof of His divinity, saluting him at first sight by his name. He told him both who he was, his name and kindred, and what title should soon be conferred upon him.

From this time, Peter and his companions became the inseparable and constant disciples of the great Messiah, submitting themselves to the rules of His discipline and living under His institutions. Then Jesus, having entered upon His important mission, thought proper to select some particular persons from among His followers to be constant witnesses of His miracles and doctrines.

They also, after His departure, might be entrusted for the care of building His Church and planting that religion in the world for which He Himself left the mansions of heaven and put on the veil of mortality.

Out of the many disciples who came to Him, He chose twelve to be His Apostles and constant attendants. These He afterward invested with the power of working miracles and sent them into different parts of Judea in order to carry on with more rapidity the great work, which He Himself had so happily begun.

We have no further account of Peter in particular till the night after our Savior's miraculously feeding the multitude in the wilderness. Jesus had ordered His Apostles to take ship and pass over to the other side while He sent the multitude away. But with a violent storm arising, they were in grave danger of their lives, when their great Master came unto them, walking on the surface of the boisterous billows with the same ease as if it had been dry ground.

At His approach, the Apostles were greatly terrified, supposing they had seen a spirit. But their compassionate Master soon dispelled their fears. Peter desired his Master to give him leave to come to Him on the water. On obtaining permission, he left the ship and walked on the sea to meet his Savior. But when he heard the deep roar around him and saw the waves increase, he began to be afraid. As his faith declined, his body sunk into the water. In greatest terror, he called for assistance to Him who was able to save.

Nor was his cry in vain; the compassionate Master stretched out His hand to again place him on the surface of the water, with this gentle reproof, "O, ye of little faith, wherefore didst thou doubt?"

Some time after, the great Redeemer, about to receive a type of His future glorification, took with Him three of His Apostles, Peter and the two sons of Zebedee. They went up into a very high mountain. While they were employed in earnest addresses to the Almighty, Jesus was transfigured before them, darting such luster from His face as exceeded the meridian rays of the sun in brightness.

After the Transfiguration, they departed the mountain and traveled through Galilee with the others. At His return to Capernaum, the tax gatherers came to Peter and asked him whether his Master was not obliged to pay tribute. When our Savior was informed of this demand, rather than give offense He wrought a miracle to pay it.

Our great Redeemer was now going for the last time to Jerusalem. He ordered two of His Apostles to fetch Him a donkey, that He might enter into the city on it, as had been foretold. Then Jesus proceeded from Jerusalem to Bethany, from whence He again sent two of His Apostles, Peter and John, to make preparations for His celebrating the Passover. Everything being ready, our Savior and His Apostles entered the house and sat down at the table.

The great Master, who often taught by example as well as precept, arose from His seat, took the towel, and pouring water into a basin, began to wash His Apostles' feet. What better way to teach them humility and charity than by His own example?

But, on His coming to Peter, he would by no means admit his Master to perform so mean and condescending an office. What! The Son of God stoop to wash the feet of a mere mortal! This thought shocked the Apostle, who strenuously declared, "Thou shalt never wash my feet!"

But Jesus told him that if He washed him not, he could have no part with Him—insinuating that this action was an ordinance. It dignified the remission of sins and the purifying virtue of the Spirit of the Most High to be poured out upon all true Christians.

Then Jesus, having set this pattern of humility, began to reflect on His approaching sufferings and on the person who would betray Him into the hands of wicked and cruel men. This traitor, who was not a stranger or an enemy, but one of His friends, one of His Apostles, and even one who now sat at supper with Him, would betray Him.

"Is it I?" they asked, with genuine sorrow. Jesus shared sop with His betrayer, then calmly excused him to go tend to his dark deed.

Our great Redeemer then began the Last Supper, that great and solemn institution which He resolved to leave behind Him. It is to be constantly celebrated in His Church as a standing monument of His love in dying for mankind. He told them at the same time that He Himself was now going to leave them, and that "whither He went they could not come."

Supper being now ended, they sang a hymn. They next departed for the Mount of Olives, where Jesus again reminded them how greatly the things He was going to suffer would offend them. They now departed for the Garden of Gethsemane. Leaving the rest of the Apostles near the entrance, our Savior, taking with Him Peter, James, and John, retired into the most solitary parts of the garden, to enter on the preparatory scene of the great tragedy that was now approaching.

Here Jesus labored under the bitterest agony that ever human nature suffered, during which He prayed with the utmost fervency to His Father. While our Redeemer was thus interceding with the Almighty, His three Apostles were fallen asleep, though He had made three separate visits to them. He called to Peter, asked him if he could not watch one hour with Him, advising them all to watch and pray that they might not enter into temptation. He added, "The spirit is, indeed, willing, but the flesh is weak."

While He was discoursing with them, a band of soldiers from the chief priests and elders, preceded by the traitor Judas to conduct and direct them, rushed into the garden, and seized the great High Priest of our faith.

Peter, whose ungovernable zeal would admit no restraint, drew his sword. Without the least order from his Master, he struck at one of the persons who seemed to be remarkably busy in binding Jesus, and cut off his right ear. This wild and unwarrantable zeal was very offensive to his Master, who rebuked Peter, then healed the wounded man.

Confused, frightened, and offended, the remaining Apostles forsook Him and fled.

The soldiers who had bound Jesus led Him away and delivered Him to the chief priests. In the meantime, Peter, who had followed the other Apostles in their flight, recovered his spirits, and returned to seek his Master.

Peter, being admitted to the hall where they had taken Jesus and being observed by the maidservant who let him in, was charged with being one of Christ's Apostles. Peter publicly denied the charge and presently withdrew into the porch. He heard a cock crow, but it was not sufficient to awaken his conscience into a quick sense of his duty and the promise he had a few hours before made to his Master that he would never deny Him.

While he continued in the porch, another maid met him and charged him with being one of the followers of Jesus of Nazareth. Peter firmly denied this and, the better to gain belief, ratified it with an oath. About an hour after this, the servant of the high priest charged him with being a disciple of Jesus. Peter, however, still denied the fact and added to his sin by ratifying it not only by an oath, but also by a solemn curse and denunciation.

But no sooner had he uttered this denial than the cock crew, at which his Master turned about and earnestly looked upon him. That look pierced him to the heart and brought to his remembrance what his Savior had more than once foretold, that he would basely and shamefully deny him.

Peter was now no longer able to contain his sorrow. He flew from the palace of the high priest, and wept bitterly.

Peter did not wait long in suspense in regard to his Lord, for on the day of His Resurrection Jesus appeared to him. As he was the first of the Apostles who had made an extraordinary confession of the divinity of the Messiah's mission, so it was reasonable he should first see Him after His Resurrection. At the same time, he was convinced that the crime he had been guilty of in denying Jesus was pardoned, and that He was come, like the good Samaritan, to pour oil into his wounded conscience.

One morning, as they were laboring at their employment, having spent the whole night without catching any fish, they saw on the shore a grave looking man, who called to them and asked them if they had any meat.

They answered, "No."

"Cast then," replied He, "the net on the right side of the ship, and ye shall find."

They followed His directions and enclosed a great number of large fish. Astonished with the remarkable success, the Apostles looked one upon another for some time, until John told Peter that the person on shore was doubtless their great Lord and Master.

Peter no sooner heard the beloved Apostle declare his opinion concerning the stranger, than his zeal took fire. Notwithstanding the coldness of the season, he put on his fisherman's coat, threw himself into the sea, and swam to shore. He was impatient to be with his dear Lord and Master, not suffering himself to stay the few minutes necessary to bring the ship to land.

As soon as the Apostles came on shore, they found a fire kindled, and fish lay upon it. Notwithstanding there were fish already on the fire, Jesus ordered them to bring of those they had caught and dress them for their meal.

When the meal was ended, our Savior addressed Himself particularly to Peter, urging him to be diligent in his care of souls. Jesus knew that nothing but a sincere love for Himself could support Peter under the troubles and dangers of so laborious and difficult a task.

The Master inquired of him whether he loved Him more than the rest of the Apostles, mildly reproving him for his denial. Peter, whom hard experience had taught humility, modestly answered that none knew so well as Jesus the integrity of his affections, "Thou knowest the hearts of all men, nothing is hid from thee, and therefore thou knowest that I love thee."

The question was three times repeated by our Savior and as often answered by the Apostle. It was right that he, who—by a threefold denial—had given so much reason to question his affection, should now—by a threefold confession—give more than common assurance of his sincere love for his Master.

To each of these confessions our great Redeemer added this extraordinary trial of Peter's affection, "Feed my sheep." Instruct and teach them with the utmost care and the utmost tenderness.

This was but one of the few interactions recorded in our canon of the many visits our Savior had with His Apostles during His 40 days of instructions (Acts 1:3). Herein is a glaring example of our canon only recording less than a hundredth part of those joyous days.

On the 40th day after His Resurrection, our Savior appeared to His Apostles in Jerusalem, this time to take His last farewell of them who had attended Him during His public ministry among the sons of men. He now led them out as far as Bethany, a small village toward the Mount of Olives.

Jesus told them that they were the persons He had chosen to be the witnesses both of His death and Resurrection, a testimony they should publish in every part of the world. Having finished this discourse, He laid hands upon them, and gave them His solemn benediction, during which He was taken from them (Luke 24:44–51; Acts 1:6–11).

The Apostles, though deprived of the personal presence of their dear Lord and Master, were untiring in fulfilling the commission they had received from Him. The first object that engaged their attention, after their return to Jerusalem, was to fill up the vacancy in their number, lately made by the unhappy fall and apostasy of Judas Iscariot.

After filling up the vacancy in the apostolic number with Matthias, they spent their time in prayer and meditation until the Feast of Pentecost, when the promise of their great Master in sending the Holy Ghost was fulfilled.

The Christian assembly were met, as usual, to perform the public services of their worship. Suddenly a sound, like that of a mighty wind, rushed in upon them, representing the powerful efficacy of that Divine Spirit which was now to be communicated to them. Afterwards there appeared small flames of fire, which, in the shape of cloven tongues, descended and sat upon the head of each of them, to denote that the enjoyment of this gift should be constant and perpetual.

Upon this, they were all immediately filled with the Holy Ghost, which, in an instant, enabled them to speak fluently several languages that they had never learned, and probably never heard. The report of so sudden and strange an action was soon spread through every part of Jerusalem, which at that time was full of Jewish proselytes, "devout men out of every nation under heaven."

These no sooner heard of this miraculous outpouring of the Holy Spirit than they flocked in large numbers to the Christian assembly. They were amazed to hear these Galileans speaking to them in their own native language, so various, and so very different from one another. This surprising transaction had different effects on the minds of the people, some attributing it to the effect of a miracle, and others to the power and strength of new wine.

Quickly, the Apostles all stood up, and Peter, in the name of the rest, undertook to refute this injurious misrepresentation. The effect of his discourse was equally superb and surprising. Vast numbers of those who before ridiculed the religion of Jesus, now acknowledged Him for their Savior, and joined with Him.

The first congregation was formally organized into a church unit with an initial membership of 3,120 members. James, the brother of Christ, became its first pastor.

Soon after this wonderful effusion of the Holy Spirit, Peter and John going up to the temple, about three in the afternoon, near the conclusion of one of the solemn hours of prayer, saw a poor impotent cripple. He was near forty years of age and had been lame from his birth. Lying at the beautiful gate of the temple, he was asking alms of those who entered the sacred edifice.

This miserable man moved their compassion. Peter, beholding him with affection, said, "Silver and gold have I none, but such as I have give I unto thee."

Then, taking the man by the hand, he commanded him, in the name of Jesus of Nazareth, to rise up and walk. Instantly the man accompanied them into the temple, walking, leaping, and praising God.

The Christian doctrine continued to be propagated without much violence or opposition in Jerusalem. But a storm of persecution against this new church soon commenced with the death of the first martyr, Stephen. Nor did it end but with the dispersion of the Apostles, by which means the glad tidings of the gospel, which till now had been confined to Judea, were preached to the Gentile world.

The storm, though violent, being at length blown over, the Church enjoyed a brief time of calmness and serenity. Peter went to visit the churches lately established in those parts by the disciples whom the persecution had dispersed. Often his companion was a young disciple named Mark (affectionately called John Mark), who recorded his clear memory of Peter's teachings in the book called Mark. That is why the Gospel of Mark is included with the three Epistles of Peter in this biography.

Peter, after having finished his visitation to the newly established churches, now returned to Jerusalem where he labored incessantly in behalf of the churches. Herod Agrippa, who had greatly pleased the Jewish hierarchy by putting the Apostle James Boanerges to death, had Peter thrown into prison soon after his return to Jerusalem.

On the very night before the day appointed for his execution, an angel was sent from heaven to the dungeon where he found Peter asleep. The angel raised him up and ordered him to put on his garments and follow him. Peter obeyed. The angel accompanied him through the streets and then departed from him.

Peter came to himself and perceived that it was no vision, but that his great and beloved Master had really sent a messenger from above who released him from prison. He hasted to the home of his companion John Mark (Acts 12:12) rather than endanger his wife and family by going to his own home. Then Peter "departed and went unto another place" (Acts 12:17).

In the morning, the officers came from Herod to the prison, with orders to bring Peter out. But when they came to the prison the keepers informed them that the

Apostle had made his escape, which so exasperated Herod that he commanded those who were entrusted with the care of the prisoner to be put to death.

By necessity, Peter could not stay in Jerusalem or Rome. Thus, we have his epistles to Babylon, the actual city itself. It was a great center of Jewish colonists. He also preached at the churches in Corinth and Antioch, as well as other churches in the Roman Empire. In the Persian Empire, Peter surely visited the strong Christian centers in Edessa (southeast Asia Minor), Arbil, Seleucia–Ctesiphon, and others. In other Asia Minor regions, Peter addressed more Church centers.

Also, there is a lot of evidence that Peter, with Paul sometimes, preached in Britain and Gaul (now France) several times.

In Gaul, Peter became the Patron Saint of Chartres, by reason of his preference to preach in the famous Druidic rock temple known as The Grotte des Druides. This is considered to be the oldest Druidic site in Gaul, on which is built the oldest cathedral in France.

Of his visits to Britain we have the corroboration of Eusebius Pamphilis (A.D. 306), whom Simon Metaphrastes (Byzantine student of saints' lives, lived in the second half of the tenth century A.D.) quotes as saying: "St. Peter to have been in Britain as well as in Rome."

Further proof of Peter's sojourn in Britain was brought to light of day in recent times when an ancient, timeworn monument was excavated at Whithorn. It is a rough-hewn stone standing four feet high by fifteen inches wide. On the face of this tablet is an inscription that reads, *Locvs Sancti Petri Apvstoli* (The Place of Peter the Apostle).

Peter was a well-traveled Apostle!

Towards the latter end of the reign of Nero (lived A.D. 37–68), when Peter was in Rome, orders were given by the Emperor for apprehending him. Ambrose (bishop of Milan, lived A.D. 340–397) tells us that when the people perceived the danger to which Peter was now exposed, they prayed him to flee Rome. Peter, with great reluctance, yielded to their entreaties, and made his escape by night.

As he passed the gate, he was met by a person in the form of his great and beloved Master. On his asking Him whither He was going, He answered, "To Rome, to be crucified a second time," to which Peter, taking this for a reproof of his cowardice, returned again into the city. He was soon after apprehended, and cast, together with Paul, into the Mamertine prison.

Here they were confined eight or nine months. During this confinement, it is generally thought that Peter wrote the second epistle to the dispersed Jews, although how he could write in such horrid conditions is hard to fathom.

Perhaps we can get a realistic impression about Peter's final days in Rome from Jowett:

> Maliciously condemned, Peter and Paul were cast into the horrible, fetid prison of the Mamertine. There, for nine months, in horrible darkness, Peter endured monstrous torture manacled to a post. Never before or since has there been a dungeon of equal horror. Historians write

Simon Peter

of it as being the most fearsome on the brutal agenda of mankind.

Over three thousand years old, it is probably the oldest torture chamber extant, the oldest remaining monument of bestiality of ancient Rome, a bleak testimony to its barbaric inhumanity, steeped in Christian tragedy and the agony of thousands of its murdered victims. It can be seen to this day, with the dungeon and the pillar to which Peter was bound in chains.

This dreaded place is known by two names. In classical history, it is referred to as Gemonium or the Tullian Keep. In later secular history, it is best known as the Mamertine. At this time, it is not out of place to pause in our story to describe this awesome pit, if only to provide us who live so securely today with a slight reminder of what the soldiers of Christ suffered for our sake, so we may be quickened the better to appreciate the substance of our Christian heritage.

The Mamertine is described as a deep cell cut out of solid rock at the foot of the capitol, consisting of two chambers, one over the other. The only entrance is through an aperture in the ceiling. The lower chamber was the death cell. Light never entered and it was never cleaned. The awful stench and filth generated a poison fatal to the inmates of the dungeon, the most awful ever known. Even as early as 50 B.C., the historian Sallust [86-34 B.C.] describes it in the following words: "In the prison called the Tullian, there is a place about ten feet deep. It is surrounded on the sides by walls and is closed above by a vaulted roof of stone. The appearance of it from the filth, the darkness, and the smell is terrible."

No one can realize what its horrors must have been a hundred years later when Peter was imprisoned in its noisome depths.

## The Triumphs of the Twelve

In this vile subterranean rock, the famed Jugurtha [North African king of Numidia from 113 B.C.] was starved and went stark raving mad before dying in 104 B.C. Vercingitorix [died 46 B.C.], the valorous Druidic Gaulish chieftain of Britain, was [held here and] murdered by the order of Julius Caesar [100-44 B.C.].

It is said that the number of Christians that perished within this diabolic cell is beyond computation—such is the glory of Rome.

One can re-read the denouncing words of the noble Queen Boadicea of Britain [died A.D. 62] with profit. She branded them for what they were. These people of the Roman purple, who scorned all their enemies as barbarian, were the greatest and most cruel barbarians of all time.

How Peter managed to survive those nine long dreadful months is beyond human imagination. During his entire incarceration he was manacled in an upright position, chained to the column, unable to lay down to rest.

Yet, his magnificent spirit remained undaunted. It flamed with the immortal fervor of his noble soul proclaiming the Glory of God, through His Son, Jesus Christ. History tells us the amazing fact that in spite of all the suffering Peter was subjected to, he converted his gaolers [jailers], Processus, Martinianus, and forty-seven others.

Peter, the Rock, as he predicted, met his death at Rome by the hands of the murderous Romans, who crucified him, according to their fiendish manner. He refused to die in the same position as our Lord, declaring he was unworthy. Peter demanded to be crucified in the reverse position, with his head hanging downward. Ironically enough, this wish was gratified by the taunting Romans in Nero's circus A.D. 67. [12]

Nero at last returned from Acaia, entered Rome in triumph, and soon after his arrival, resolved that the Apostles should fall as victims to his cruelty. The Christians in Rome were continually offering up their prayers to heaven to protect those two holy persons (Peter and Paul).

But the Almighty was now willing to put an end to their sorrows, after sealing the truth they had preached with their own blood, to receive them into the regions of eternal bliss and happiness. They exchanged their crowns of martyrdom for the crowns of glory. Accordingly, the cruel Emperor of Rome condemned them both to their morbid fates in A.D. 67.

Peter having taken his farewell of the brethren, especially of Paul, was taken from the prison and led to the top of the Vatican Mount, near the Tiber. There he was accused by Simon Magus, a sorcerer, then sentenced, with his wife in Nero's Circus, to surrender his life upon the cross. He was forced to watch his wife being led out to her martyrdom first. He called out comfort to her and ended with these words, "O thou, remember the Lord!"

He then insisted he be crucified head downwards, as he did not consider himself worthy to be hanged in the same manner as his Master.

Peter's sainted body was removed to the cemetery in the Appian Way, two miles from Rome. There it rested obscurely until the reign of Constantine (A.D. 306–337). He built a church over the cemetery site and reburied Peter's bones to honor this saint. (Since this biography was penned in 1884, the bones of Peter have been found.)[13]

# Commentary on the First Epistle of Peter

The Empire's condemnation put a peculiar strain upon the churches all over the Roman world. The ignorant masses already regarded Christianity as depraved and vicious. They also falsely credited them with eating human flesh and other monstrous practices. Worse, the Empire had ruled that being a Christian was a crime punishable by death. Thus, the Christian had neither the protection of the state nor the sympathy of his fellows.

In this situation, Peter wrote to his brethren throughout Asia Minor a letter of advice and encouragement. Perhaps the Epistle to the Hebrews had already reached Rome and its ringing challenge to the Romans to be teachers stirred him to write.

Peter styles himself as a witness of Christ's sufferings, that is, one who had risked his life by acknowledging his faith before the authorities. He had to stay out of Jerusalem and Rome to stay alive. Thus, Peter could not pastor the Head Church at first. It is all the more inspiring when he sends to the Christians of the chief provinces of Asia Minor a message of hope.

This group already enjoys a salvation of unutterable worth and have awaiting them in heaven an imperishable inheritance. Their present trials are only to prove and refine their faith.

As Christians, they are to live lives of holiness and love. By their pure and unobjectionable conduct, they must disarm the public suspicion of their practices. They must obey the Emperor and his appointed governors.

Government is for the restraint of evildoers and for the encouragement of good. The example of Christ's sufferings should encourage servants when they are mistreated, to imitate His patience and self-command. All must cultivate sympathy, humility, and love.

No one can reasonably molest them if they live uprightly, but if they should suffer for their very righteousness, they would only be the more blessed. It is better to suffer for well doing than for evil doing.

They must not be afraid, but be ready to give respectful and honest answers to magistrates who examine them. By their uprightness of life, they will silence and condemn popular false statements. Christ, too, suffered to bring them to God. They must live the new Christian life that He opened to them, not their old gross heathen life of sin.

The fiery trial to which they are now exposed must not be thought strange. Through it, they may share in Christ's sufferings and, therefore, in His coming glory as well. It is a privilege to endure reproach for the name of Christ.

To be punished for committing crime carries disgrace along with it, but to endure punishment for being a Christian does honor to God. They can only commit their lives to God and keep on doing what is right.

Their elders must do their work in a noble and high-minded way, as true shepherds of the flock of God under the Chief Shepherd, Christ. They must all humble themselves under God's mighty hand and He will in His good time lift them up again through His grace.

Everywhere their Christian brethren are being compelled to endure this same bitter experience. God is the source of all their help and, after they have suffered the buffetings of persecution for a little while, He will give them deliverance.

Among the messages, which conclude the letter, is one from the Church at Rome in which Peter identified himself as an elder. He gave the imperiled Christians all through Asia Minor a message of hope and courage during the persecution of Emperor Domitian (ruled A.D. 81–96). He pointed out the difference between suffering for being a criminal and suffering for being a Christian. Lastly, he inspired them to overcome the hatred and slanders of the heathen world by lives of purity and goodness.

# Commentary on the Second Epistle of Peter

A generation after a vigorous letter of Jude was written, it was taken over almost word for word into what we know as Second Peter. In the early part of the second century, various books began to be written in Christian circles about the Apostle Peter, or even in his name, until one could have collected a whole New Testament bearing his name. This would have yielded a Gospel of Peter, the Acts of Peter, the Teaching of Peter, the Preaching of Peter, the Epistles of Peter, and the Revelation of Peter. Most of these laid claim to being from the pen of Peter himself.

The one that most insistently claims Peter as its author is our Second Peter. It comes out of a time when Christians seriously doubted the Second Coming of Jesus. A number of years perhaps had passed since Jesus' ministry, and men were saying, "Where is His promised coming? For from the day the Fathers fell asleep, all things continue as they were from the beginning of creation."

The spiritualizing of the Second Coming, which the Gospel of John wrought out, did not hold the same view that Peter writes of. Rather, he prefers to meet the skepticism of his day about the Second Coming with a sturdy insistence on the old doctrine. In support of it, he appeals to the Transfiguration, and to the widespread ancient belief that the universe is to be destroyed by fire.

He repeats the denunciation, which Jude hurled at the Gnostic libertines of his day, only it is now directed against those who are giving up the expectation of the Second Coming. Jude has some hope of correcting and saving the persons he condemned, but Peter has no hope about those whom he attacks.

He supports his exhortations by an appeal to the letters of Paul. He evidently knows a number of them, for he speaks of "all his letters." He considers them scripture and says that many misinterpret them, to their own spiritual ruin.

This view of the letters of Paul, combined with the use in Second Peter of other New Testament books, proves its date of writing to be the latest book in the New Testament. It was not addressed to any one church or district, but was published as a tract or pamphlet to correct the growing disbelief in the Second Coming of Jesus.

⁂

# Commentary on the Gospel According to Mark (Peter)

Peter was dead. The impulsive Apostle who had followed Jesus about Galilee and who had lived to share in the worldwide Gentile mission had met his death in Rome with his good wife and Paul. With Peter dead, another chief link the Roman Church had had with the earthly ministry of Jesus was gone.

The familiar stories and reminiscences of Jesus' words and doings would no longer be heard from the lips of the chief Apostles. East and west alike had heard them, but in the restless activity of the Gentile mission, and especially in the general expectation of Jesus' speedy return, no one had thought to write them down.

But there still lived in Rome a younger man who had for some time attended the old Apostle. When Peter preached in his native Aramaic to little companies of Roman Christians, he had stood at his side to translate his words into Greek. His name was Mark, affectionately called John Mark.

In his youth, he had gone with Paul and Barnabas on their first missionary journey to Cyprus. Then he had disappointed and even offended Paul by withdrawing from the party when they had landed in Pamphylia (a country in southeast Asia Minor) to push on into the treacherous mountains of Asia Minor. Mark had afterward gone a second time to Cyprus with Barnabas, to whom he was closely related.

Through the years that had passed since then, he had probably kept in close touch with the Christian leaders at Antioch (modern "Antakya" in southeast Asia Minor) and at Jerusalem, where his mother's house had been from the first a center for the Christian community. It was probably as Peter's companion that he had made his way at length to Rome, and, there until Peter's martyrdom, had served the old Apostle as his interpreter.

Mark saw at once the great loss the churches would sustain if Peter's recollections of Jesus perished. At the same time, he saw a way to preserve at least the best part of them for the comfort and instruction of the Roman believers.

He had become so familiar with Peter's preaching, through his practice of translating it, that it was possible for him to remember and write down much that Peter had been wont to tell about his walks and talks with Jesus in Galilee and Jerusalem more than thirty years before.

In this way, Mark came to write what we call the Gospel of Mark. But Mark did not call it his gospel; indeed it is not certain that he called it a gospel at all. If he had thought of naming its author he would quite certainly have called it Peter's work rather than his own. But the order and the Greek dress of the gospel are the work of Mark, however much he is indebted to his memory of Peter's sermons for the facts that he reports.

In the selection of what he should record, Mark was doubtless often influenced by the conditions and needs of the Roman Christians for whom he wrote. But it is Peter's picture of Jesus that he preserves, just as Peter would have drawn it, yet with a skill in story telling which may be Peter's own.

We see Jesus go out to John the Baptist from his home among the hills of Galilee. After Jesus directed baptism at John's hands, He became immediately possessed with the Spirit of God and filled with a divine validation of His commission as God's Anointed to establish God's kingdom in the world.

When John's work is cut short, Jesus begins preaching in Galilee. Marvelous cures accompany His preaching, and the Galileans soon throng Him wherever He goes. His freedom in dealing not only with Pharisaic tradition but also with the precepts of the Law itself soon brings Him into conflict with the Pharisees. Their increasing opposition before long threatens His life.

After two or three withdrawals from Galilee, probably for reasons of security or leisure to plan His course, Jesus at length declares to His Apostles His purpose of going up to Jerusalem to the springtime Feast of the Passover. He warns them that the movement will cost Him

His life, but declares that God will, after all, save Him and raise Him up.

Bewildered and alarmed, they follow Him through Peraea (section of territory east of the Jordan River) up to Jerusalem. He enters in triumph, now for the first time declaring Himself the Messiah by riding into the city in the way in which Zechariah had said the Messiah would enter it, on a donkey—as a Jewish King would. The Romans perceived no threat to their power as their emperors rode on horses.

Jesus boldly enters the temple and drives out of its courts the privileged dealers in sacrificial items who had made it their market place. The Sadducees, who control the temple and profit by these abuses, have Him arrested on the night of the Passover.

Up to the final hours before His arrest, Jesus tenderly showed the Apostles how to bring the presence and peace of the kingdom of God into their own lives on earth.

After His arrest and illegal hasty examinations in late night before Jewish authorities, they hurry Him at dawn to Roman authorities to facilitate His execution.

The book more than once predicts His Resurrection. In its complete form, it doubtless contained a brief account of His appearance to the two Marys and Salome after his burial. It had by the beginning of the second century lost its original ending. Whole new conclusions have been used in different manuscripts to complete it. The original one, probably only ten or twelve lines long, has never been certainly restored.

## The Triumphs of the Twelve

As lightly as Mark's Gospel was esteemed in the ancient Church in comparison with the richer works of Matthew and Luke, no more convincing or dramatic account has been written of the sublime and heroic effort of Jesus to execute the greatest task ever conceived—to set up the kingdom of God on earth through His perfect life culminating in His atoning sacrifice.

# James

*And when his disciples James and John saw [this], they said, Lord, wilt thou that we command fire to come down from heaven, and consume them, even as Elias did? . . . For the Son of man is not come to destroy men's lives, but to save them.*

—Luke 9:54, 56

# JAMES

This Apostle, who was surnamed "the Great," by way of distinction from the other James, was a cousin to Jesus. His father was Zebedee; and his mother was Salome, sister to Mary, the mother of Jesus. James was by trade a fisherman. He applied himself with diligence and was exercising his employment when the Savior of the world—passing by the Sea of Galilee—saw him with his brother in the ship, and called them both to be His disciples.

They cheerfully complied and immediately left all to follow Him. They readily delivered themselves up to perform whatever services He should appoint them. When family calls, you respond.

Soon after this, James was called from the station of an ordinary disciple to the apostolic office. He was further honored with some particular favors beyond most of the Apostles, being one of the three whom our Lord made choice of as His companions in the more intimate transactions of His life.

Thus, with Peter and his brother John, James attended his Master when He raised the daughter of Jarius from the dead. This gave them courage later in their lives to face death with absolute peace.

They were admitted to Christ's glorious Transfiguration on the Mount. This helped them to know the reality of the spiritual world with absolute knowledge.

When Jesus was to undergo His bitter agonies in the garden, as preparatory sufferings to His Passion, the three of them were taken to be absolute witnesses of them. This helped them understand that they, too, must suffer agony for Christ. Then, as the first of these three mortals to die a martyr's death for their Master, it is significant that Jesus permitted him to share the intimate secrets of these three events.

Jesus also gave them new nicknames: James and John, who were brothers, Boanerges, or the Sons of Thunder; and Simon He called Peter, or "a rock." Some think that these names were given to them on account of their loud and bold preaching of the gospel to the world, fearing no threatenings, despising all opposition, and going on thundering in the ears of a drowsy and sleepy world.

They roused and awakened the consciences of listeners with the earnestness and power of their preaching, which resembled thunder, just as the voice of God powerfully shakes the natural world and breaks in pieces the cedars of Lebanon. Others think it relates to the doctrines they delivered, teaching the great mysteries and promulgating the gospel in a more profound and lofty strain than the rest.

Our Savior, doubtless, alluded by these nicknames to the naturally furious and resolute disposition of these two brothers, who seem to have been of a more fiery temper than the rest of the Apostles. For instance, when our Lord was on His journey to Jerusalem, He sent some of His disciples before Him to make preparations for His coming. On their entering a village of Samaria, James and John were rudely rejected by reason of an old grudge that existed between the Samaritans and the Jews. Also, our Savior, by going up to Jerusalem, seemed to slight their place of worship on Mount Gerizim.

These trivial excuses for rudeness and inhospitality were so highly resented by James and John that they came to Jesus desiring to know if He would not imitate Elias by calling down fire from heaven to consume this barbarous, inhospitable people.

Thus, we find that the best of men are but men, and that mankind's corrupt nature will sometimes appear even in renewed minds. But Jesus soon convinced them of their mistake by telling them that instead of destroying, He was come to save the lives of the children of men.

Sophronius (Patriarch of Jerusalem, lived A.D. 560–638) tells us that, after the Ascension of Jesus, this Apostle preached to the dispersed Jews, that is, to those converts who were dispersed after the death of Stephen. The Spanish writers affirm that, after preaching the gospel in several parts of Judea and Samaria, he visited Spain, where he planted Christianity and appointed some select disciples to perfect what he had begun.

If we consider the shortness of James' life and that the other Apostles continued in a body at Jerusalem even after the dispersion of the other Christians, we find it difficult to allow time sufficient for so tedious and difficult a voyage as going to Spain was in those early ages. Therefore, it is safest to confine his ministry to Judea and the adjacent countries.

Herod, who was a bigot to the Jewish religion, as well as being desirous of acquiring the favor of the Jewish hierarchy, began a violent persecution of the Christians. His zeal against them animated him to pass sentence of death on James immediately.

As James was led to the place of execution, his accuser, Hermagenes, having been converted by that remarkable courage and constancy shown by the Apostle at the time of his trial, repented of what he had done, came and fell down at the Apostle's feet, and heartily begged his pardon for what he had said against him.

"Peace," replied James, "my son, peace be unto thee, and pardon of thy faults." Upon which the officer publicly declared himself a Christian, and both were beheaded at the same time. Thus fell the great Apostle James, being the first who had gained his martyr's crown. He drank cheerfully of that cup of which he had long since told his Lord he was ready to drink (see Mark 10:39).

# John the Beloved

*For God so loved the world, that he gave his only begotten Son, that whosoever believeth in him should not perish, but have everlasting life. For God sent not his Son into the world to condemn the world; but that the world through him might be saved.*

—John 3:16–17

# JOHN
## THE BELOVED

John, who was surnamed "the Beloved," was a cousin to Jesus through his mother, Salome. With his brother James, he searched for the light of truth. From the very minute and circumstantial account this Apostle gives of John the Baptist, he is supposed to have been one of his followers.

John is also thought to be that "other disciple," who, in the first chapter of the gospel, is said to be present with Andrew when John declared Jesus to be "the Lamb of God." Thereupon he followed Him to the place of His abode.

He was by much the youngest of the Apostles, yet he was admitted into as great a share of his Master's confidence as any of them. He was one of those to whom Jesus communicated the most private transactions of His life.

John was one of those whom Jesus took with Him when He raised the daughter of Jarius from the dead. He displayed a specimen of His divinity to him in His Transfiguration on the Mount; John was present at His conference with Moses and Elias and heard that voice from heaven that declared Him the most beloved Son of God. Lastly, John was one of those who were His companions in His solitude, most retired devotions, and bitter agonies in the Garden of Gethsemane.

These instances of particular favor our Apostle endeavored, in some measures, to answer by returns of particular kindness and constancy. At first, he deserted his Master upon His arrest. Yet, he recovered himself and came back to see his Savior. He confidently entered the high priest's hall, followed our Lord through His trial, and at last waited on Him at His execution with Jesus' mother—owning Him, as well as being owned by Him— in the midst of armed soldiers, and in the thickest crowds of his most persistent enemies.

Here it was that our great Redeemer committed to his care His sorrowful and disconsolate mother with His dying breath. Certainly, Jesus could not have given a more honorable testimony of His particular respect and kindness to John than by leaving His own mother to his trust and care.

After the Ascension of the Savior, when the Apostles made a division of the provinces amongst themselves, that of Asia fell to the share of John. He did not immediately enter upon his charge, but continued in Jerusalem until the death of Mary, which might be from fifteen to thirty years after the Lord's Ascension. Being released from the trust committed to his care by his dying Master, he traveled into Asia and industriously applied himself to the propagation of Christianity.

John preached where the gospel had not yet been known and confirmed where it was already established. Many churches of note and eminence were founded by him, particularly those of Smyrna (modern Izmir, Turkey), Pergamus, Thyatira (modern Akhisar, Turkey), Sardis (in modern Manisa province of Turkey), Philadelphia (western Turkey), Laodicea (southwest Turkey), and others. His chief place of residence was at Ephesus, where Paul had, many years before, founded a church and made Timothy the bishop of it.

After spending several years in Ephesus, accusations were made against John to Emperor Domitian (ruled A.D. 81–96), who had begun a persecution against the Christians. He was an eminent asserter of atheism and impiety and a public subverter of the religion of the empire.

The proconsul sent him bound to Rome where he met with the treatment that might have been expected from so barbarous a prince, being thrown into a cauldron of boiling oil. But the Almighty, who reserved him for further services in the vineyard of His Son, restrained the heat, and delivered him from this seemingly unavoidable destruction.

Surely one would have thought that so miraculous a deliverance should have been sufficient to have persuaded any rational man that the religion he taught was from

God, and that he was protected from danger by the hand of Omnipotence. But miracles themselves were not sufficient to convince this cruel emperor or abate his fury. He then ordered John to be transported to an almost desolate island in the Archipelago, called Patmos.

There he continued several years instructing the poor inhabitants in the knowledge of the Christian faith. About the end of Domitian's reign, John wrote his book of Revelation, exhibiting, by visions and prophetical representations, the state and condition of Christianity in the future periods and ages of the Church.

Upon the death of Domitian and the succession of Nerva (reigned A.D. 96–98), who repealed all the odious acts of his predecessor, and, by public edicts, recalled those whom the fury of Domitian had banished, John returned to Asia and fixed his seat again at Ephesus. This despite that the people of the city had lately martyred Timothy, their bishop.

Here, with the assistance of seven other bishops, he took upon himself the government of the large region of Asia Minor. He managed the clergy in the best manner that the circumstances of those times would permit, in an indefatigable execution of his charge. He traveled from east to west to instruct the world in the principles of the holy religion he was sent to propagate.

In this manner, John continued to labor in the vineyard of his Master until he supposedly died in the beginning of Trajan's reign (A.D. 98–117?), in the ninety-eighth year of his age. According to Eusebius, his remains were buried near Ephesus. However, there is support in the book of John that he was commissioned to serve his Master until the Second Coming (John 21:21–23). This is further confirmed in the Book of Mormon (3 Nephi 28:6) and in the Doctrine and Covenants (D&C 7).

John seems always to have led a single life, though some of the ancients tell us he was a married man. He was polished by no study or arts of learning, but what was wanting from human art was abundantly supplied by the excellent faculties of his mind and a fullness of divine grace, with which he was adorned.

His humility was admirable, studiously concealing his own honor. In his epistles, he never styles himself as either Apostle or evangelist; the title of presbyter, or elder, is all he assumes and probably in regard to his age as much as his office.

In his Gospel, when he speaks of "the disciple whom Jesus loved," he constantly conceals his own name leaving the reader to discover whom he meant. Love and charity he practiced himself and affectionately pressed upon others. The great love of his Savior towards him seems to have inspired his soul with a larger and more generous charity than the rest.

This charity is the great vein that runs through all his writings, especially his epistles, where he urges it as the great and peculiar law of Christianity. Without charity, all other pretences to the religion of Jesus are vain and frivolous, useless, and insignificant. This was his constant practice.

When age and the decays of nature had rendered him so weak that he was unable to preach to the people any longer, tradition says, he was gently helped to the Church at Ephesus, and always repeated to them the same precept, "Little children, love one another."

When his hearers wearied of the constant repetition of this same thing, they asked him why he never varied his discourse. He answered, "Because to love one another was the command of the Savior, and consequently one grand guide of our conduct through life. He that loveth his brother abideth in the light, and there is no occasion of stumbling in him. But he who hateth his brother is in darkness, and walketh in darkness, and knoweth not whither he goeth, because that darkness hath blinded his eyes."

The greatest instance of our Apostle's care for the souls of men is in the writings he left to posterity. The first in time, though placed last in the order of canon, is his Apocalypse, or book of Revelation. He wrote it during his banishment to the isle of Patmos.

Next to the Apocalypse, in order of time, are his three Epistles, the first of which is universal, intended for all times and all places. It contains the most excellent rules for the conduct of a Christian life. It presses one to holiness and pureness of manners, and not to be satisfied with a naked and empty profession of religion. Do not be led away with the crafty insinuations of seducers, it warns. Men are cautioned against the poisonous principles and practice of the Gnostics.

The Apostle here, according to his usual modesty, conceals his name, it being of more consequence to wise men what is said rather than about who says it. It appears from Augustine (A.D. 354–430) that this Epistle was anciently inscribed to the Parthians, because, in all probability, John preached the gospel in Parthia (Iran and parts of surrounding countries).

The other two Epistles are but short, and directed to particular persons. One is to a lady of great quality; the other to the charitable and hospitable Gaius, the kindest and the most courteous entertainer of all indigent Christians.

Before John undertook the task of writing his Gospel, he caused a general fast to be kept by all the Asiatic churches, to implore the blessing of heaven on such a great and momentous undertaking. When this was done, he set about the work. He completed it in so excellent and sublime a manner that the ancients generally compared him to an eagle soaring aloft among the clouds whither the weak eye of man was not able to follow him.

"Among all the evangelical writers," says Basil (bishop of Caesarea, A.D. 330–379), "none are like John, the Son of Thunder, for the sublimity of his speech, and the height of his discourses, which are beyond any man's capacity to fully reach and comprehend."

"John, as a true Son of Thunder," says Epiphanius (A.D. 320–403), "by a loftiness of speech peculiar to himself, acquaints us, as it were, out of the clouds and dark recesses of wisdom, with the divine doctrine of the Son of God."

# Commentary on the Gospel According to John

John was one of the first Apostles Jesus called to His ministry. He continued to reside at Jerusalem after the Ascension of the Lord to care for Mary, His mother. Later he removed, it is believed, to Ephesus (west Asia Minor), about A.D. 65, where he exercised a powerful influence in spreading Christianity through Asia Minor.

About A.D. 95, he was banished by the Emperor Domitian to the isle of Patmos, where he had the visions described in the book of Revelation. He afterwards returned to Ephesus, where he supposedly died in the third year of Trajan, A.D. 100, being then, according to Epiphanius, ninety-four years of age (although Eusebius lists him as 98 years of age on page 77). However, newly revealed canon indicates he was granted his desire to serve his Master until His Second Coming (D&C 7).

Ephesus and Patmos are claimed by various writers as the place at which this Gospel was written. The weight of evidence seems to weigh in favor of Ephesus. Probably the date of the Gospel was about A.D. 78.

The contents of the Gospel may be arranged in the following order:

1. The Prologue (John 1:1–18)
2. The History (John 1:19–20:29)
   a) Various events relating to our Lord's ministry, narrated in connection with eight journeys (John 1:19–12:50)

(1) Into Judea, and beginning of His ministry (John 1:19–2:12).

(2) Appearance at the Passover in the first year of His ministry (John 2:13–4); the manifestation of His glory in Jerusalem (John 2:13–3:21); and in the journey back (John 3:22–4).

(3) In the second year of His ministry, about the Passover (John 5).

(4) About the Passover, in the third year of His ministry, beyond Jordan (John 6). His glory is shown by the multiplication of the loaves, by His walking on the sea, and by the discourses with the Jews, His disciples, and His Apostles.

(5) Six months before His death, began at the Feast of Tabernacles (John 7–10:21). Circumstances in which the journey was undertaken (John 7:1–13); five signs of His glory shown at Jerusalem (John 7:14–10:21).

(6) About the Feast of Dedication (John 10:22–42); His testimony in Solomon's Porch and His departure beyond Jordan.

(7) In Judea towards Bethany (John 11:1–54). The raising of Lazarus and its consequences.

(8) Before His last Passover (John 11:55–12). Plots of the Jews; His entry into Jerusalem and the temple.

b) Events of the death of Christ (John 13–20:29)
(1) Preparation for His Passion (John 13–17). Last Supper, discourse to His disciples, His commendatory prayer.
(2) The circumstances of His Passion and death (John 17–19). His apprehension, trial, and Crucifixion.
(3) His Resurrection and the proofs of it (John 20:1–29).
c) The Conclusion (John 20:30–21:1)
(1) Scope of the foregoing history (John 20:30–31).
(2) Confirmation of the authority of the Apostle by additional historical facts, and by the testimony supposed to be that of the elders of the Church (John 21:1–24).
(3) Reason for the termination of the history (John 21:25).

The 25$^{th}$ verse, and the latter half of the 24$^{th}$, John 21, are generally received as an undisguised addition, probably by the elders of the Ephesian Church, where his Gospel was first published.

The introduction of John's Gospel is so very different from those of the other evangelists that we may be certain some peculiar circumstances induced the venerable writer to pursue the course that he did. The doctrine of Christ's divinity is so intimately connected with all the great and distinguishing truths of the Christian religion, that we cannot wonder that John become anxious to set this mystery in as clear a light as possible.

To an unsophisticated mind, the luminous statements of John on this doctrine will appear bright as a sunbeam. Further, the attempts of some modern writers to put a new gloss upon them will excite at least our pity, if not our contempt, especially as productions of learned men.

"In the beginning was the Word, and the Word was with God, and the Word was God . . . All things were made by him; and without him was not any thing made that was made. In him was life, and the life was the light of men. And the light shineth in darkness; and the darkness comprehended it not" (John 1:1–5).

Neither is the introduction to this Gospel its only peculiarity. The evangelists, whose writings had preceded John, had taken but little notice of our Lord's teaching and actions from the commencement of His ministry and before the imprisonment of John the Baptist. Our Apostle, therefore, supplied what had been previously omitted.

He, moreover, is accustomed to pass over accounts that had been before mentioned. The genealogy of our Savior's humanity having been stated both by Matthew and Luke, John illustrates Christ's divinity while refuting the errors of Cerinthus (Gnostic teacher who flourished about A.D. 100) and other early heretics.

John's Gospel, without causing any discrepancy with the other evangelists, presents to us much of what is not found elsewhere:

- The account given of Nathanael, in John 1.
- The miracle of the conversion of water into wine at the marriage in Cana of Galilee, as recorded in John 2.
- The lengthened conversation between Jesus and Nicodemus, in which the Savior so clearly illustrates the nature of the new birth, or regeneration, as mentioned in John 3.
- The important interview with the woman of Samaria at Jacob's well, as recorded in John 4, in which the Redeemer distinctly avows himself to be the Messiah, "I that speak unto thee, am He."

To John we are, moreover, indebted for the narrative of the woman taken in adultery, recorded in the eighth chapter. The force of conscience in inducing her accusers to go out one by one—"beginning at the eldest even unto the last," when "Jesus was left alone, and the woman standing in the midst"—is powerful.

The Savior, having enquired, "Hath no man condemned thee?" was pleased to pronounce her acquittal; "Neither do I condemn thee; go and sin no more."

The interesting narrative of the man who was born blind and his subsequent recovery, by anointing the eyes of the blind man with clay and causing him to wash in the pool of Siloam, is peculiar to John 9.

How beautifully does John illustrate the power and grace of Christ toward this individual. On meeting him again and finding that he had been excommunicated by the Jews, He inquires, "Dost thou believe on the Son of God?"

He answered and said, "Who is He, Lord, that I might believe on Him?" And Jesus said unto him, "Thou hast both seen Him, and He it is, that talketh with thee."

First, it is Luke who introduces us to the family of Martha and Mary. To John alone, however, are we indebted for the afflictive scenes of Bethany, following the death of Lazarus, brother of the pious women, Mary and Martha. Few narratives even of sacred story can be compared with that, which is found in John 11.

The intimacy existing between Christ and the family enabled Him to throw, so to speak, His whole soul into the mournful events at Bethany. The energy of Martha in promptly meeting her divine Lord and the quiet resignation of Mary in remaining in the house are beautifully portrayed by John.

With such feeling does John record the interview between Christ and the afflicted Martha. "Lord," she exclaimed, "if thou hadst been here, my brother had not died; but I know that even now, whatsoever thou wilt ask of God, God will give it thee." Jesus said unto her, "Thy brother shall rise again."

To John we are again indebted for another introduction to the lovely family of Bethany, recorded in John 12. "Mary took a pound of ointment of spikenard very costly," valued by the traitor Judas at three hundred pence, "and anointed the feet of Jesus, and wiped them with her hair."

At the Last Supper, the long discourse of Jesus with His disciples, after He had instituted the Holy Supper and the departure of Judas the traitor from amongst them, as recorded in John 14–17, we alone owe to this excellent writer.

The concluding chapters of the same Gospel contain this matter, new and peculiar, respecting the trial, sufferings, and death of the Son of God. John was the only Apostle who witnessed all of these last tragic scenes of his divine Redeemer's life.

Further, John gives a clearer account of the Savior's different visits to Jerusalem than the other evangelists. We learn that the Savior commemorated the Feast of the Passover for four successive years, forming the full term of His public ministry.

In reference to the style of John's writings, we may remark that most of them, more especially the Gospel, bear strong internal marks of being the work of an unlearned Jew.

The Gospel, at least, must have been published at a time and in a country where the people, in general, knew very little of Jewish rites and manners. Hence, those who in the other Gospels are called simply the people or the multitude, are, by John, denominated the Jews. This would be inappropriate if employed in Judea or its vicinity.

So again, it was customary in the East, both with Jews and others, to use proper names independently significant, which, when they went abroad, were translated into the language of the country. So that there might be no mistake of the person's meaning, John was careful, when the Greek name was prevalent, to mention both names, both Syriac and Greek:

- Peter was called Cephas (John 1:43).
- "Thomas, which is called Didymus" (John 11:16).

The same may be observed of some titles in current use:

- Rabbi, which signifies doctor (John 1:38).
- Messiah, a term equivalent to Christ (John 1:41).
- The water-pots are said to be placed after the Jewish rites of cleansing (John 2:6).
- The Passover also, once and again, is designated the Jewish Passover (John 2:13; 6:4).

This style runs through the whole Gospel, showing that though the writer was a Jew, yet for the sake of being understood by foreigners (to whom he wrote) he employed this redundant phraseology.

Testimonial emphasis eminently distinguishes all of John's writings. It is indeed common to all the evangelists, but to John in particular.

There are wonderful things in John's style that are too remarkable to be overlooked. He endeavors to impress important truths more strongly on the minds of his hearers by employing, at once, an affirmative and a negative proposition:

- "All things were made by him, and without him was not any thing made, which was made" (John 1:3).
- "He confessed, and denied not, but confessed" (John 1:20).

Poetic repetitions are also frequent with our Evangelist:

- "He was not that light, but was sent to bear witness of that light" (John 1:8).
- "In the beginning was the Word, and the Word was with God, and the Word was God. The same was in the beginning with God" (John 1:1–2).

Hebraisms (Hebrew terms) may be found in all the evangelists, but some abound more with one sort of Hebraism and others, with another.

An idiom very common to our Evangelist, is the repetition, or introduction, of the personal pronoun in cases wherein it is perfectly redundant:

- "Upon whom thou shalt see the Spirit descending and remaining on him" (John 1:33), and
- "He it is, who coming after me, is preferred before me, whose shoe's latchet I am not worthy to unloose" (John 1:27).

John also is peculiar in the application of some names, as, the words, "and the Only Begotten," applied to the Lord Jesus Christ, and "of the Comforter," to the Holy Spirit.

The phrase "verily, verily," is never employed by the other evangelists, being found only in the writings of John.

With these peculiarities, the writings of our Evangelist form an invaluable part of the New Testament, particularly his Gospel. It has always been admired by the church universal, for the explicit statements of divine truth, and for a simple and affectionate style.

# Commentary on the Letters of John

About the beginning of the second century, a disagreement arose among the Christians of Asia. It was about the reality of the life and death of Jesus. How could the Messiah, the Son of God, possessed of a divine nature so utterly removed from earthly matter, have lived a life of human limitation and suffered a shameful and agonizing death?

It was a favorite idea in ancient thought that the material universe was intrinsically evil, or at least opposed to goodness, and that God, being wholly good, could not come into any direct contact with it. Such contact, it was thought, would infect God with the evil inherent in all matter.

Some Christians who at the same time accepted Jesus as the divine Messiah held this idea. From this contradiction, they escaped in part by claiming that Jesus' divine nature or messiahship descended on Him at His baptism and left Him just before His death on the cross. They inferred that His sufferings were only seeming and not real. From this idea, they were known as Docetists, that is, "seemists."

The Docetists were probably better educated to begin with than most Christians. Their profession of these semi-philosophical views of Christ's life and death still further separated them from the ordinary people. This separation was increased by the claim they made of higher enlightenment, closer mystic fellowship with God, clearer knowledge of truth and freedom from sin, no matter what they did.

Expressions like "I have fellowship with God," "I know him," "I have no sin," "I am in the light," were often on their lips. Both their spiritual pretensions and their fantastic view of Christ made them an unwholesome influence in the Asian churches. More than one Christian writer was aroused to dispute their claims.

John was a leader of such influence and reputation that he could, in his correspondence, style himself simply as "the Elder." Wide as his influence must have been, there were some who withstood his authority and refused to further his enterprises.

With his approval, missionaries had gone out through Asia to extend the gospel among the Greek population. Some Christians had welcomed them hospitably and helped them on their way. However, others, who were hostile to the Elder, had refused to receive them and had threatened any who did so with exclusion from the Church.

In this situation, the Elder writes two letters. One, known to us as Third John, is to a certain Gaius. He is asked to acknowledge his support, encourage him to continue it, and to warn him against the party of Diotrephes. Gaius is probably the most influential of the

Elder's friends and supporters in his own community, while Diotrephes is the leader of the party hostile to the Elder. The letter is probably delivered by Demetrius, one of the missionaries in question.

At the same time, the Elder writes another short letter, our Second John, to the church to which Gaius belongs, urging its members to love one another and to live harmoniously together. It also warns them against the deceivers who teach that Christ has not come in the flesh. They are to let the advocates of this teaching severely alone, refusing them even the ordinary salutations and the hospitality usual among Christians.

The two letters are brief, for the Elder is coming to them very soon in person. But, as short as they are, they bring us into the very heart of a controversy that was already dividing individual churches and threatening the peace of a whole district.

As missionaries like Demetrius went about the province of Asia, under the Elder's direction, they took with them a longer letter from his pen in which the same pressing matters were more fully presented. We have seen that the short letters are without his name, and the long letter bears not even his title.

It hardly required it if it was to be carried by his messengers and read by them as from him in the assembled churches they visited. This longer letter, known to us as First John, deals with the same question as Second John. It takes the same view of the matter and puts it with confident authority. But the situation has developed somewhat, for the Docetists, or some of them, have now left the Church.

The Elder begins with the most confident emphasis. His own experience guarantees the truth of his message, which he is sending in order that his readers may share the fellowship with God and Christ that he enjoys.

The heart of that message is that God was historically manifested in the life of Christ. The Christian experience is fully sufficient for anyone's spiritual needs. To claim fellowship with God and then to live an evil life will not do; the claim is false. The Docetic pretension to sinlessness is mere deceit. The Christian way is to own one's sins and seek forgiveness.

The claim of knowing Christ is meaningless apart from obedience to His commands. Living as He lived is the only evidence of union with Him. Those who claim peculiar illumination and yet treat their brethren with exclusiveness and contempt show that they have never risen to a truthful Christian attitude.

The Elder's reason for writing to his friends is that they have laid the foundation of real Christian experience. He would warn them against sinking again into a life of worldliness and sin.

The breach with the Docetic thinkers, with their claims of freedom from sin, is complete. It is well that they have left the Church, for they have no right to be in it. Those who deny that Jesus is the Christ are not Christians but anti-Christs.

In opposition to their teachings, true Christians

should continue to cultivate that spiritual experience upon which they have entered. They must abide in Christ and follow the guidance of the Spirit. They are to seek, as children of a righteous Heavenly Father, to be righteous like Him. Righteousness and love are the marks of the Christian life. Jesus, in laying down His life for us, has shown what love may be.

Some who urge the Docetic teaching claim that the Holy Spirit in their hearts has endorsed it. But the Spirit of God authorizes no such teaching. Only spirits that confess that Jesus Christ is come in the flesh are of God. Spirits that deny this are of the world. The Elder declares that he is of God, and that all who really know God will obey his solemn warning against these spirits of anti-Christ.

Love is the perfect bond in all this great spiritual fellowship. Love is of God and God is love. He has shown it by sending His Son into the world to give us life. We love because He first loved us. If He so loved us, we also ought to love one another.

Belief in Jesus as the Christ is the sign of sonship to God and the way to the life of love, since it is the manifestation in Jesus of God's love that kindles love in us.

The messiahship of Jesus is evidenced not only by the voice of the Spirit, but by His human life and death. There are three who bear witness, the Spirit, the water, and the blood. The witness is this, that God has given us eternal life and this life is in His Son. To have eternal life, we must see in Jesus the Christ the indispensable revelation of God.

The Elder writes to confirm his readers in their assurance of eternal life. Sonship to God means the renunciation of sin. The Christian has an inward assurance that he belongs to God, whom Jesus has revealed. Here is the true God and eternal life.

Except for a few touches that mark it very definitely as a letter (1 John 2:12–14), this little work might pass for a sermon. It is clearly a circular letter written to save the churches of Asia from the Docetic views that threatened them.

The great words of the letter, life, light and love, figure importantly in the Fourth Gospel also. In its meditative and yet tersely witty style, the letter resembles the Gospel.

It has been said that while the Gospel argues that Jesus is the Christ, the letter contends that the Christ is Jesus, that is, the Messiah is identical with the historical Jesus.

Who was this Asian "elder" who could so confidently instruct and command the churches of the countryside? To John the letters have always been ascribed. We may think of the Elder John as sending them out from Ephesus, one to Gaius, one to the Church to which he belonged, and to other churches, in full assurance that the Christian experience and belief in Jesus as the Christ would save them from the mistakes of Docetism.

# Commentary on the Revelation of John

It was a dangerous thing in the first century to be a Christian. Jesus himself had laid down His life for His cause, and many of the Apostles met their deaths as martyrs, that is, witnesses, to the new faith. Although Christianity was not yet a "licensed" or "permitted religion," yet to be a Christian was not against the Roman law.

Through the first century, we can trace the Christians' hope that, when at length the Roman government should decide what its attitude toward Christians was to be, the decision would be favorable. Luke points out that Pilate himself was disposed to release Jesus and expressly says that neither Herod nor Pilate found any fault in Him.

Luke also brings out the fact that the proconsul Gallio at Corinth would not even entertain a charge against Paul. At Caesarea both Agrippa and the procurator Festus declared that Paul might have been released if he had not appealed to the Emperor.

Paul had encouraged his converts to honor the Emperor and obey the law. In Second Thessalonians, Paul had referred to the Emperor as a great restraining power, holding the forces of lawlessness in check.

Nero's (A.D. 54–68) savage outbreak against the Roman Church must have startled and appalled Christians all over the world. But that attack, though severe, was short, and left the status of Christians before the law undecided as before. Nero's victims suffered under the charge of burning the city of Rome, not from being Christians. Paul and Peter, as Luke indicates, were tried and probably executed as agitators, not as Christians.

It is clear that representative Christians like Luke kept hoping that when a test case arose, the Empire would not condemn the Christian movement and put Christians under its ban.

But these hopes were doomed to disappointment. Late in the reign of Domitian (A.D. 81–96), the emperor-worship which had prevailed in some parts of the Empire since the time of Augustus (27 B.C.–A.D. 14) began to threaten the peace of the churches.

Earlier emperors had, for the most part, let it take its course, but Domitian found divine honors so congenial that he came to insist upon them. There was an obvious political value in binding together the heterogeneous populations of the Empire, differing in speech, race, civilization, and religion, by one common religious loyalty to the August Imperator. Most Asiatic peoples found this easy. While worshiping numerous gods, they did not much object to accepting one more.

With the Christians, it was very different. Their faith forbade such an acknowledgement. The scattered churches of Asia, where the matter first became acute, now witnessed the disappointment of their cherished hope of freedom to worship God undisturbed, in their own way.

It is hard to realize all that this meant to them. Their early teachers had been mistaken. The Empire was not their friend and safeguard, to be loyally obeyed. It now suddenly appeared in its true colors as their bitter and unrelenting foe. It inexorably demanded from them a worship of the Emperor that the Christians must refuse to obey.

The Christians and the Empire were finally and hopelessly at war.

The Christian leaders of Asia must have realized this with stricken hearts, forcing them to view the history of the Christian movement from a new point of view. But what else could they have expected? Jesus, Paul, and Peter had suffered death for the kingdom of God, and at the hands of Rome.

In Nero's day, hundreds of other Christians had perished in Rome at the Emperor's bidding. The Empire, as they now saw, had long recorded its verdict. It was against them.

The matter of worshiping the Emperor came home to the Christians of Asia in various forms. His name and likeness appeared on many of the coins they used. He had among them his provincial priesthood, charged with the maintenance of his worship throughout Asia.

Christians might be called upon, as Pliny (Roman writer, A.D. 23–79) tells us, to worship the image of the Emperor. It was customary to attest legal documents—contracts, wills, leases, and the like—with an oath by the fortune of the Emperor.

Refusal to make this sworn endorsement would at once involve one in suspicion and lead to official inquiries as to the apparent disloyalty of the person to the imperial government.

Why not then make the oath? It was after all a purely formal matter with all who used it. Why not simply add to one's business documents, as everyone did, the harmless words, "And I make oath by the Emperor Domitianus Caesar Augustus Germanicus that I have made no false statement"?

So slight an accommodation might seem a very excusable way to gain security and peace.

Yet, even in slight concessions to pagan practice, the Christian leaders of Asia saw a serious peril. There must be no compromise. The Church might perish in the conflict, but the conflict itself could not be avoided. The Church must brace itself for the struggle, and compromising was not the way to begin.

On the contrary, the Church must absolutely disavow everything pertaining to the wicked system through which the devil himself was now assailing it. In the Empire, the Asian Christians now recognized not a beneficent and protecting power but an instrument of Satan.

Among the first victims of the kindling persecution was a Christian Prophet of Ephesus, named John. He seems to have been arrested on the charge of being a Christian and banished to the neighboring island of Patmos, perhaps condemned to hard labor.

He could no longer perform for his Asian fellow-Christians the Apostle's work of edification, comfort, and consolation described by Paul in First Corinthians, though they needed it now as never before. But he might hope to reach them by letters.

As John wrote these to the seven leading churches of Asia, his message expanded into a book. He uses the cryptic symbolic forms of the old Jewish Apocalypses, of Daniel or Enoch, in which empires and movements figure in the guise of beasts and monsters. The slow development of historical forces is pictured as vivid personal conflict between embodiments of rival powers.

Indeed, John's message is one that may not be put in plain words, because it contains a bitter attack upon the government under which the Apostle and his readers live.

The canon of the writings of the prophets had long been regarded by Jews as closed. Anyone who wished to put forth a religious message as a work of prophecy had therefore to assume the name of some ancient patriarch or prophet. However, the Christians believed the prophetic spirit to have been given anew to them. Thus, a Christian prophet had no need to disguise his identity. John in Patmos writes to the neighboring churches as their brother, who shares with them the agony of the rising persecution.

The task of the exiled prophet was to stiffen his brothers in Asia against the temptations of apostasy and compromise that the persecution would inevitably bring. John aroused their faith.

In the apparent hopelessness of their position, a few scattered bands of humble people arrayed against the giant worldwide strength of the Roman Empire, they needed to have shown to them the great eternal forces that were on their side and insured their final victory. In this conflict, Rome was not to triumph, but to inevitably perish.

The Prophet's letters to the seven churches convey to them the particular lessons that he knows they need. But one note is common to all the letters "To him that overcometh," to the victor in the impending trial, the Prophet promises a divine reward.

This is only the beginning of his message. Caught up in his meditation into the very presence of God, the Prophet in the Spirit sees Him, as Isaiah saw Him, enthroned in ineffable splendor. In His hand is a roll crowded with writing and sealed seven times to shut its contents from sight.

Only the Lamb of God proves able to unfasten these seals and unlock the mysterious Book of Destiny, which seems to contain the will of God for the future of the world. The scrolls need to be opened in order to be realized.

Dreadful plagues of invasion, war, famine, pestilence, and convulsion attend the breaking of the successive seals, doubtless reflecting familiar contemporary events in which the Prophet sees the beginning of the end.

On the opening of the seventh seal, seven angels with trumpets stand forth and blow, each blast heralding some new disaster for mankind. Despite these warnings, men continue in idolatry and wickedness. The seventh trumpet at length sounds and proclaims the triumph of the kingdom of God, to which the Prophet believes all the miseries and catastrophes of his time are leading.

The victory is thus assured, but it has yet to be won. The Prophet now sees the dragon Satan engaged by the archangel Michael and the heavenly armies. Defeated in heaven, the dragon next assails the Saints upon the earth. In this campaign, Satan has two allies, one from the sea—the Roman Empire—the other from the land—the Emperor cult of Asia.

Again the Prophet's vision changes. Seven bowls symbolizing the wrath of God, now at last irrepressible, are poured out on the earth. An angel shows him the supreme abomination sitting on seven hills and drunk with the blood of the saints. Another angel declares to him its doom, over which kings and merchants lament, while a thunderous chorus of praise to the Lord God Omnipotent arises from the redeemed.

The Prophet's thought hastens on from the fate of the persecutioners and the imprisonment of Satan to the glorification of those who have suffered martyrdom rather than worship the Emperor. As priests of God, they reign with Christ a thousand years, until the great white throne appears, and the dead, small and great, stand before it for the Final Judgment.

These lurid scenes of plague and convulsion now give way to the serene beauty of the new heavens and the new earth, with the New Jerusalem coming down out of heaven from God who makes all things new. Amid its glories, God's servants, triumphant after their trial and anguish, serve Him and look upon His face.

The Prophet begins with a blessing upon anyone who shall read his prophecy and upon those who shall hear it read. He closes with a warning against any tampering with its contents. This warning was periodically used by earlier biblical writers in their books (see Deuteronomy 4:2; 12:32 and Proverbs 30:5–6). Also, John wrote his Revelation before he wrote his other books, not after. Thus, John's warning has reference only to the Revelation and not to the Bible as a whole.

The book is clearly intended to be read at Christian meetings. By its repeated claim of prophetic character, and in its zeal to make its message heard, it also claims the inspiration of scripture. It is thus, in a real sense, the nucleus of the New Testament collection.

The Revelation is not a loyal book. Its writer hates the Roman government and denounces its wickedness in persecuting the Church in unmeasured terms, which every Christian of the day must have understood. It does not indeed advise rebellion, but it is, from an official Roman point of view, a seditious and incendiary pamphlet.

But so symbolic and perplexing is its language that few outside of Jewish or Christian circles could have understood its meaning, or guessed that by "Babylon" the Prophet meant the "Roman Empire." Its value to the frightened and wavering Christians of Asia must have been great, for it promised them an early and complete deliverance, and cheered them to steadfastness and devotion.

Their trial indeed proved less severe than they had feared, for twenty years later, Ignatius (lived A.D. 35–117?) found these same churches strong and earnest. Forty years after the writing of Revelation, a Christian convert named Justin found this book still prized by the Ephesian Church. Ignatius and Justin both suffered martyrdom in Rome and joined the army of those who had come out of great tribulation, having made their robes white in the blood of the Lamb.

In these successive conflicts and through many more down to the present day, Christians have cheered themselves in persecution and high-souled courage of the banished Prophet of Ephesus. John the Beloved of Jesus Christ shows us how to look in the face of hopeless defeat and destruction with a faith that looked through death. In stirring and immortal pictures, he assured his troubled fellow Christians of the certain and glorious triumph of the kingdom of God.

# Book of Revelation Outlined

"Blessed is he that readeth, and they that hear the words of this prophecy . . . for the time is at hand" (Revelation 1:3).

From *ScriptureKIT Book 1* by Bruce Barton

| Chapters | Seal | Description |
|---|---|---|
| 1:1–8 | | John (the beloved disciple and author of the Gospel of John and books First, Second, and Third John) bears witness of the truthfulness of this revelation. |
| 1:9–20 | | Christ gives special instructions to John. |
| 2:1–3:22 | | The message delivered by an angel is to the Saints in the seven churches in Asia about events to transpire in the future. God knows what will happen and cannot be surprised. |
| 4:1–11 D&C 77:1–5 | | A vision of heaven. John sees Heavenly Father and Jesus in celestial heaven. |
| Chapters 5–20 D&C 77:6–7 | | A vision of the history of the world. John sees a complete history of the world— past, present, future—revealed as each of the seven seals is opened. |
| | | The Seven Seals (The seven 1000-year "days" of the earth's temporal existence.) |
| 6:1–2 | 1 | From about 4004 B.C. to 3000 B.C. Includes Adam's life and Enoch's ministry. |
| 6:3–4 | 2 | From 3000 to 2000 B.C.; includes Noah and the Flood and Tower of Babel. |
| 6:5–6 | 3 | From 2000 to 1000 B.C.; includes Abraham; Jacob (Israel); Joseph; the Exodus from Egypt. |

| Chapters | Seal | Description |
|---|---|---|
| 6:7–8 | 4 | From 1000 B.C. to birth of Christ, including Isaiah; "Loss" of the Ten Tribes, Babylonian captivity of Judah. |
| 6:9–11 | 5 | From Christ's birth to A.D. 1000, including John the Baptist; life of Christ; death of Apostles; great Apostasy. |
| 6:12–17 | 6 | From A.D. 1000 to 2000, including the Renaissance and Reformation; Restoration; great signs and calamities. |
| 7:1–8 D&C 77:8–11 | 6 | Zion is established and the gospel preached to the four corners of the world. |
| 7:9–17 | | John sees those saved in Christ's kingdom. |
| 8:1 D&C 77:12; 88:93–96 | 7 | The earth's Sabbath starts with sanctifying Earth though destruction, fire, and bloodshed. |
| 9:1–21 D&C 77:13 | 7 | This chapter describes the great Battle of Armageddon before the Second Coming of Christ. |
| 10:1–11 D&C 77:14 | | The "little book" is delivered and read. Between the sounding of the sixth trumpet and the vision of the two witnesses in Jerusalem, an angel delivers a book to John and commands him to read it. |
| 11:1–14 D&C 77:15 | 7 | John learns of the two prophets in Jerusalem and their role. |
| 11:14–19 | 7 | The great millennium is ushered in with the Second Coming of Christ. Christ reigns personally upon Earth and the wicked are destroyed. |
| 12:1–14:20 | | The kingdom of God and Satan's kingdom. |
| 12:1–17 | | The War in Heaven, which began there in our premortal state, continues on Earth. |

# The Triumphs of the Twelve

| Chapters | Seal | Description |
|----------|------|-------------|
| 12:1–17 (cont.) | | John sees the Church organized at the time of Christ, and its collapse. The spiritual darkness that follows is beheld along with the warfare that started in heaven between Satan's side and the earth's people. |
| 13:1–18 | | The kingdom of Satan. John sees various kingdoms receiving power from Satan to fight God and His work. |
| 14:1–20 | | The final outcome. John sees Christ's coming and the Restoration of the gospel by an angel (Moroni), both before and after Christ's Second Coming. Destruction of the wicked and harvest of the righteous observed. |
| 15:1–4 | | John sees those saved in God's kingdom. Just before pouring out of vials of judgment, John is shown the multitude of those who overcome the beast praising God and the Lamb. |
| 15:5–16:21 | 7 | The wicked receive their collapse through seven plagues, more about the Battle of Armageddon, and three great changes in the earth's surface. |
| 17:1–18:27 | | The destruction of Satan's kingdom. After the seven vials of judgment have been poured out, an angel explains the symbolism of the great whore (symbolic representation of Satan's kingdom and the counterpart of the true Church, the bride of Christ). The world laments in great sorrow the fall of Satan's empire. |
| 19:1–10 | 7 | Songs of glory in heaven proclaim fall of Babylon and triumph of God's kingdom. |

| Chapters | Seal | Description |
|---|---|---|
| 19:11–21 | 7 | Christ comes as King of Kings! The Supper of the Great God. |
| 20:1–3 | 7 | Satan bound for 1,000 years during Millennium. |
| 20:4–6 | 7 | Saints live and reign during Millennium. |
| 20:7–10 | 7 | Satan loosed; final battle of Gog and Magog; Satan banished forever. |
| 20:11–15 | 7 | The great and last judgment of the wicked. |
| 21:1–22:5 | | A vision of the celestial earth; John sees the earth returned to its paradisiacal state. |
| 22:6–15 | | Angel bears witness of truthfulness of vision. Christ gives special instructions to John. |
| 22:16–21 | | A final word of counsel and admonishment to the Saints. God is in control at all times. We must trust Him! |

# Matthew

*As Jesus sat at meat in [Matthew's] house, behold, many publicans and sinners came and sat down with him and his disciples. And when the Pharisees saw it, they said unto his disciples, Why eateth your Master with publicans and sinners? But when Jesus heard [that], he said unto them, They that be whole need not a physician, but they that are sick.*

—Matthew 9:10–12

# MATTHEW

In his own Gospel, Matthew is not ranked immediately after the preceding Apostle but numbers
himself eighth on the list after his associate, Thomas. All
the other lists agree in giving this Apostle a place immediately after Nathanael.

In connection with this Apostle, as in other instances,
there is a serious question about his name and individual
identity. This is because of the different names under
which he is mentioned in different parts of the sacred
record. In his own Gospel, he is referred to by no other
name than his common one. In Mark and Luke, the circumstances of his call are narrated with the details similar
to those recorded about the same event by himself. Matthew (called in the same manner and form of words used
in summoning the other Apostles) is named Levi, the son
of Alpheus. Then Mark and Luke record Matthew by his
common name among the Twelve in the list of names.

Some have thought that the circumstance of their
mentioning Matthew in this manner, without referring
at all to his identity with the person named Levi, proves
that they had no idea that the former name was applied

to the same person as the latter. On the contrary, they may have been detailing the call of some other disciple—perhaps Jude, who is also called by the similar name, Lebbeus, and is thought to have been the son of Alpheus. This view is not improbable and is so well supported by coinciding circumstances as to throw great uncertainty over the whole matter.

The circumstances of his call, as narrated by himself, are represented as occurring at or near Capernaum. "Jesus, passing out of the city, saw a man named Matthew sitting at the receipt of custom, and He said to him, 'Follow me.' And he arose and followed Him" (Matthew 9:9).

This account shows Matthew's occupation, which is also known from the title of "tax gatherer," annexed to his name, in the list of Apostles. This was an occupation with a source of great profit to those employed in it. Consequently, it was much sought after. It was also connected with a great deal of hatred, from the relation in which they stood to the Jews in this profitable business.

The class of collectors to which Matthew belonged, in particular, being the mere tax gatherers, sat to collect the money, penny by penny. The unwilling people, whose national pride was every moment wounded by the degrading *foreign* acts of violence by the Romans, caused Matthew to suffer embarrassment.

Tax gatherers were believed to have renounced all patriotism and honor—in stooping for the base purposes of pecuniary gain—to act as instruments of such a galling form of servitude. His own people therefore treated

Matthew daily with a universal, popular hatred and scorn.

A class of men thus deprived of all character for honor and delicacy of feeling would naturally grow hardened beyond all sense of shame. Out of this hated class, Jesus did not hesitate to take at least one—perhaps more—of those whom He chose for the express purpose of building up a pure faith and of evangelizing the world.

No doubt, before the occasion of this call, Matthew had been a frequent hearer of the words of truth, which fell from the divinely eloquent lips of the Redeemer. Surely, these words had not been without a purifying and exalting effect on the heart of the publican, though long degraded by daily and hourly familiarity with meanness and vice.

So weaned was his soul from the love of the gainful pursuit to which he had been devoted, that at the first call from Jesus, he arose from the place of toll gathering and followed his summoner. He embarked on a duty for which his previous occupation had but poorly prepared him.

With such satisfaction did he renounce his old vocation for the apostleship of the Nazarene that he made it a great occasion of rejoicing. He celebrated the day as a festival. He called in all his old friends as well as his new ones, to share in the hospitable entertainment that he spread for all who could join with him in his social circle.

Nor did the Redeemer despise the rough and indiscriminate company to which the grateful Matthew had invited Him. Rather, He rejoiced in an opportunity to do good to a class of people so seldom brought under the means of grace. He unhesitatingly sat down to the entertainment—Savior and sinners, toll gatherers and Apostles—all thronging in one diverse group around the festive board.

What a sight this was for the proud Pharisees who were spitefully watching the conduct of the Nazarene who had lately taken upon Himself the exalted character of a teacher and a reformer of the law!

Passing into the house with the throng, they saw the much glorified Prophet of Nazareth sitting at the social table along with a parcel of low customhouse collectors, toll gatherers, tidewaiters, and cheats—one of whose fraternity He had just adopted into the goodly fellowship of His Apostles. Jesus was now eating and drinking with these outcast villains, without repelling the familiar merriment even of the lowest of them.

At this spectacle, so degrading to such a dignity as they considered most becoming in one who aspired to be a teacher of morals and religion, the scribes and Pharisees sneeringly asked the disciples of Jesus, "Why eateth your Master with tax gatherers and sinners?"

Jesus, hearing the malicious inquiry, answered it with such a touch of irony as best suited its impertinence. "They that be whole need not a physician, but they that are sick. But go ye and learn what that meaneth, 'I will have mercy, and not sacrifice;' for I am not come to call the righteous, but sinners to repentance " (Matthew 9:11–13).

After the history of his call, not one circumstance is related respecting him, either in the Gospels, or Acts, or the epistles. In his own Gospel, Matthew makes not the slightest allusion to anything either said or done by himself, nor does his name anywhere occur except in the apostolic lists. It is only in the noble record that he has left of the life of Christ, in the Gospel that bears his name, that any monument of his actions and character can now be found.

Yet, this solitary remaining effort of his genius is of such importance in the history of revealed religion, that hardly the most eminent of the Apostles is so often brought to mind as this Apostle. His clear, simple, but impressive testimony to the words and deeds of his Lord now stands at the head of the New Testament.

On the history of this portion of the Christian scriptures, the very earliest testimony on this point dates within seventy-five years of the time of Matthew himself. It expressly declares that Matthew wrote his Gospel in the Hebrew language, and that each one interpreted it for himself.

It is also said, on somewhat early authority, that he wrote his Gospel when he was about to depart from Palestine so that those whom he left behind might have an authentic record of the facts of the life of Christ. The point seems well established that Matthew wrote in

Hebrew. However, what now exists as his Gospel is a translation into the Greek, made by some of the disciples.

After the Greek translation was admitted, the Hebrew copy was chiefly owned and used by the Nazarai, a middle sect between Jews and Christians. With the former, they adhered to the rites and ceremonies of the Mosaic law. With the latter, they believed in Christ and embraced His religion. Hence, this Gospel has been styled in two ways as, "the gospel according to the Hebrews," and "the Gospel of the Nazarenes."

William Steuart McBirinie's book, *The Search for the Twelve Apostles* best explains the various accounts of Matthew's death. "There are so many traditions which seem to be mutually contradictory that one can but list them all and try to make a synthesis of them as Barclay has done:"

> Socrates said that Matthew was allotted Ethiopia in the apostolic comity agreement (The E.H., 1, 19; cf. Rubinus, 1,9). Ambrose connects him with Persia, Paulinus of Nola with Parthia, Isidore with Macedonia.
>
> Clement of Alexandria indicates he died a natural death (*The Miscellanies,* 4, 9). Clement says he was a vegetarian eating seeds, nuts, and vegetables without flesh. The *Talmud* says that Matthew was condemned to death by the Jewish Sanhedrin.
>
> The apocryphal *Acts of Andrew and Matthew,* which later was put into Anglo-Saxon verse, claims that he was sent to the cannibalistic Anthropophagi who attempted to put his eyes out and put him in prison for 30 days before

eating him. On the 27th day, he was rescued by Andrew who came by sea, miraculously escaping a storm, and thus rescued Matthew. Matthew returned to the Anthropophagi, working miracles among them, and the king became jealous of him. They bound Matthew, covered him with papyrus soaked in dolphin oil, poured brimstone, asphalt, and pitch upon him, heaped up tow and wood and surrounded him with the golden images of the 12 gods of the people. But the fire turned to dew and the flames flew out and melted the images. Finally, the fire took the form of a dragon, chased the king into his palace, and curled around about him so that he could not move. Then Matthew rebuked the fire and prayed and gave up the ghost. The King was converted and became a priest and with two angels, Matthew departed into heaven. [*The Master's Men*, William Barclay, 66–68]

According to E. J. Goodspeed in *Matthew, Apostle and Evangelist*, there was a confusion in the early stories between Matthias and Matthew. The tradition of the *Babylonian Talmud* (Sanhedrin 43 a.) tells of the trial and execution of one "Matthai." Matthew probably did not die in the same country as Matthias.

The difficulty in knowing for certain the countries which Matthew probably visited lies in the identification of the country known as "Ethiopia." The Ethiopia in Africa is well known to us, but there was also an Asiatic "Ethiopia" which was south of the Caspian Sea in Persia (now Iran). It was in the kingdom of the Parthians, but from all accounts was off the well-traveled trade routes.

As we have seen, Ambrose links Matthew with Persia.

The associations of Thomas with a "Gospel of Matthew" which was reputedly found in India are well known. This would seem to indicate at least a tradition of the Apostle Matthew as having been near the Asiatic "Ethiopia." It would have been natural for a copy of Matthew's Gospel to have found its way to India if Matthew himself had been in Persia (now Iran), which he probably indeed did visit, for Persia was on the direct trade route from Antioch to India.

# Commentary on the Gospel According to Matthew

The Christian movement had failed in its first campaign. The nation in which it had arisen and to which its founder belonged had disowned it. It was as though the Israelites had refused Moses. This was the more staggering because the gospel had been represented by Jesus' early followers as the crown and completion of Judaism.

Jesus was to be the Jewish Messiah through whom the nation's high hopes of spiritual triumph were to be realized. But the Jews had refused to recognize in Him the long-expected Deliverer and had disclaimed His gospel. Who was right? The prophets had anticipated a redeemed and glorified nation, but the nation had refused to be redeemed and glorified by such a Messiah. The divine program had broken down.

Yet, the gospel was not failing. Among the Greeks of

the Roman Empire, it was having large and increasing success. Strangers were taking the places that the prophets had expected would be occupied by their own Jewish countrymen. The Church was rapidly becoming a Greek affair.

The Gentiles had readily accepted the Messiah and made Him their own. To a Christian thinker of Jewish training, this only increased the difficulty of the problem. For how could the messiahship of Jesus be harmonized with the nation's rejection of Him? The prophets had associated the messianic deliverer with the redeemed nation, but the events of history had disappointed this hope.

What did it mean? Were the prophets wrong, or was Jesus not the Messiah? Paul had seen the difficulty and in writing to the Romans had proposed a solution. It was in effect that the Jews would ultimately turn to the gospel, and so all Israel would be saved.

Yet, since the writing of the epistle to the Romans, the breach between Jews and Christians had widened. Paul's solution seemed more improbable than ever.

But an event had now happened which put a new aspect on the matter. Jerusalem had fallen. The downfall of the Jewish nation put into the hand of the Apostle Matthew the key to the mystery. Jesus was the Messiah of the prophets!

He had offered the kingdom of heaven to the Jews, finally presenting Himself as their Messiah before the assembled nation in its capital at its great annual feast. Misled by its religious leaders, the nation had rejected

Him and driven Him to His death. But in this rejection it had condemned itself. Therefore, God had rejected Israel, and the kingdom it had disowned had been given to the nations.

In the fall of Jerusalem, Matthew saw the punishment of the Jewish nation for its rejection of the Messiah. In this fact was now the proof that the gospel was intended for all nations.

The vehicle for this striking and timely philosophy of early Christian history was to be a book. It may be called the first book of Christian literature, for Paul's writings, great as they are, are letters, not books. Likewise, Mark, for all its value, is hardly to be dignified as a book in the sense of a conscious literary creation.

This book was to tell the life of the Messiah, which should articulate the gospel with the Jewish scriptures and legitimize the Christian movement.

For this purpose, a variety of materials lay ready for Matthew's hand. The narrative of Mark was familiar to him. He had also a collection of Jesus' sayings, which he may have noted, and one or two other primitive documents of mingled discourse and incident.

The mere possession of these partial and unrelated writings was in itself a challenge to harmonize and even combine them, just as our Four Gospels have, ever since their origin, invited the harmonist and the biographer.

With a freedom and a skill that are alike surprising, Matthew has wrought these materials into the first life of Christ. Perhaps it might better be called the first historic apology for universal Christianity, for it is a biography with a purpose.

Jesus, though legally descended from Abraham through the royal line of David, is really begotten of the Father through the Holy Spirit, a symbol at once of His sinlessness and His sonship.

Divinely acknowledged as Messiah at His baptism and victorious over Satan in the temptation conflict, He declares His message in a series of great sermons. He sets forth in each some notable aspect of the kingdom of heaven.

In the first of these, the Sermon on the Mount, Jesus demands of those who would enter the new kingdom a righteousness higher than that based by the scribes upon the Jewish law. He follows this bold demand with a series of prophetic and messianic acts that show His right to make it. The Jewish leaders are unconvinced and quickly become hostile.

His nearest Apostles, at length, recognize in Him the Messiah, and He welcomes this expression of their faith. Soon afterward, they gain a new idea of the spiritual and prophetic character of His messiahship through the Transfiguration experience. They see Him associated with Moses and Elijah, the great prophetic molders of the Jewish religion.

Already foreseeing the fatal end of His work, Jesus yet continues to preach in Galilee. At length He sets out for Jerusalem to put the nation to the supreme test of accepting or refusing His message. They refuse it, and He predicts the nation's doom in consequence.

The kingdom of God shall be taken away from them and given to a nation that brings forth the fruits thereof. The last discourses denounce the wickedness and hypocrisy of the nation's religious leaders. They predict the doom of the city and nation, to be followed shortly by the triumphant return of the Messiah in judgment.

The Jewish leaders, offended at His claims of authority, cause His arrest and execution. Yet, on the third day, He reappears to some women of the Apostles' company and afterward to the Apostles repeatedly for 40 days. He charges them to carry His gospel to all the nations.

Jesus had expressly confined His own work and that of his Apostles, during His life, to the Jews. Since they had refused the gospel, His last command to His followers was to offer it henceforth to all mankind. The curtain falls on the Gospel of Matthew, leaving Jesus an abiding presence with His Apostles.

The Jewish war of A.D. 66–70 culminated in the fall of Jerusalem and the destruction of the last vestige of Jewish national life. It must have brought what Jesus had said of these things powerfully before His followers' minds and shown them a welcome solution for the problem that perplexed them.

Jesus had not come to destroy the Law or the Prophets. His work and its fortunes stood in close relation with them. But, as between the Jewish Messiah and the Jewish nation, the verdict of history had gone for the Messiah and against the nation. The nation had already perished while He was coming to be worshiped all over the Greek world.

The obviousness of this solution to our minds is simply an evidence of the Apostle's success in grappling with the problem. We owe to him the solution that seems so simple and complete. Few any longer stop to think that a triumphant Messiah, apart from a triumphant nation, is hardly hinted at in the Old Testament.

In this, as in other respects, the success of the book was early and lasting. As a biography of the Messiah, it swept aside all the partial documents its author had used as his sources. Most of them perished—among them the "Sayings Attributed to Matthew the Apostle"—probably because Matthew had wrought into his book everything of evident worth that they contained.

Even what we call the Gospel of Mark seems by the narrowest margin to have escaped destruction through neglect. Its escape is the more to be wondered at since practically all that it offered to the religious life of the early Church had been taken up into this new life of Christ.

For the probably Jewish-Christian circle for which it was written, the new book performed a threefold task. It solved, by its philosophy of Christian history, their most serious intellectual problem. It harmonized and unified their diverse materials relating to Jesus' life and teaching. And it did these things with an intuitive sense for religious values that has given it its unique position ever since.

Forty years after it was written, it was quoted at Antioch as "the Gospel," being probably the first book to bear that name.

Twenty years later, when the Ephesian leaders put together the Four Gospels, the first place among them was given to it and its name was extended to the whole group. A new designation had therefore to be found for it, so it was distinguished as "according to Matthew," probably in recognition of that apostolic record in which it was believed to be based.

There has been much discussion as to the language in which it was originally composed. It must, however, be observed that every early writer who mentions that Matthew wrote a Gospel *at all* says that he wrote it in Hebrew (that is, in the Syro-Chaldaic) and in Palestine in the first century.

Moreover, every early writer that has come down to us uses the *Greek* version of Matthew and this with the definite recognition that it is a translation. Hence, we may be sure that the Greek copy belongs to the Apostolic Age, having been thus authoritatively used from and up to that time.

The principal divisions of the Gospel are:
1. The introduction to the ministry of Christ (Matthew 1–4).
2. The laying down of the new Law for the Church in the "Sermon on the Mount" (Matthew 5–7).
3. Events in historical order, showing Him as the worker of miracles (Matthew 8–9).
4. The appointment of apostles to preach the kingdom (Matthew 10).
5. The doubts and opposition excited by His activity

in divers minds, in John's disciples, in sundry cities, in the Pharisees (Matthew 11–12).

6. A series of parables on the nature of the kingdom (Matthew 13).

7. Similar to 5, the effects of the ministry on His countrymen, on Herod, on the people of Gennesaret, scribes and Pharisees, and on multitudes whom He feeds (Matthew 13:53–16:12).

8. Revelation to His disciples of His sufferings; His instructions to them (Matthew 16:13–18:35).

9. Events of a journey to Jerusalem (Matthew 19–20).

10. Entrance into Jerusalem, resistance to Him there, and denunciation of the Pharisees (Matthew 21–23).

11. Last discourses; Jesus as Lord and Judge of Jerusalem, and also of the world (Matthew 24–25).

12. Passion and Resurrection (Matthew 26–28).

# Andrew

*One of the two which heard John [speak], and followed him, was Andrew, Simon Peter's brother. He first findeth his own brother Simon, and saith unto him, We have found the Messias, which is, being interpreted, the Christ.*

—John 1:40-41

# ANDREW

This Apostle was born at Bethsaida, a city of Galilee, built on the banks of the lake of Genesareth (Sea of Galilee), and was son to Jona or Jonas, a fisherman of that town. He was brother to Simon Peter, but whether older or younger is not certainly known, though the generality of the ancients intimate that he was the younger. He was brought up in his father's trade, at which he labored till our Savior called him to be a fisher of men.

John the Baptist had lately preached the doctrine of repentance, and was, by the generality of the Jews, held in great veneration. He was esteemed for the impartiality of his precepts and the remarkable strictness and austerity of his life. In the number of his followers was our Apostle. He had accompanied him beyond Jordan, when the Messiah, who had before been baptized, came again that way.

Upon his approach, the Baptist pointed him out as the Messiah, styling Him, "the Lamb of God," the true sacrifice that was to expiate the sins of the world. As soon as the Baptist had given this character of Jesus, Andrew and another disciple, probably John Boanerges, followed the Savior of mankind to the place of His abode.

After some conversation with Him, Andrew departed to find his brother Peter. He informed Peter that he had discovered the great Messiah, so long expected by the house of Jacob.[14] Accordingly, they came to Jesus.

Possibly up to a year after, Jesus, while passing through Galilee, found Andrew and Peter fishing on the Sea of Galilee. He fully satisfied them of the greatness and divinity of His person by a miraculous draught of fishes, which they took at His command.

Jesus now told them that they should enter on a different series of labors. Instead of fish, they should, by the ability and influence of their doctrine upon the heart and conscience, catch men. Jesus commanded them to follow Him as His immediate Apostles and attendants. Accordingly, they left all and followed Him.

After the Ascension of Jesus into heaven and the descension of the Holy Ghost on the Apostles, to qualify them for their great undertaking, Andrew was chosen to preach the gospel in Scythia (a country in southeast Europe) and the neighboring countries. Accordingly, he departed from Jerusalem. He first traveled through Cappadocia (a region of northeast Asia Minor), Galatia (central Asia Minor), and Bithynia (a Roman province in north Asia Minor), instructing the inhabitants in the faith of Christ. He continued his journey along the Euxine Sea (Black Sea) into the deserts of Scythia.

An ancient author tells us that he first came to Amynsus, where, being entertained by a Jew, he went into the synagogue and preached to them concerning Jesus. From the prophecies of the Old Testament, he proved Jesus Christ to be the Messiah and Savior of the world. Having converted many here, he set up the times for public meetings and ordained them priests.

He went next to Trapezium, a maritime city on the Euxine Sea. From whence, after visiting many other places, he came to Nice, where he stayed two years, preaching and working miracles with great success. After leaving Nice, he passed to Nicomedia (northwest Asia Minor), and from thence to Chalcedon (still in northwest Asia Minor), whence he sailed through the Propontis, came by the Euxine Sea to Heracles, and afterward to Amastria (north Asia Minor).

In all these places he met with the greatest difficulties but overcame them by invincible patience and resolution. He next came to Sinope (northeast Asia Minor), a city situated from the same sea and famous for both the birth and burial of King Mithradates. Here he met with his brother Peter and stayed with him a considerable time.

The inhabitants of Sinope were mostly Jews, who, partly from a zeal for their religion and partly from their barbarous manners, were exasperated against Andrew. A confederacy was formed to burn the house in which he lodged.

Being disappointed in their design, they treated him with the most savage cruelty. After throwing him on the ground, they stamped upon him with their feet, pulling and dragging him from place to place. Some beat him with clubs, some pelted him with stones, and others, to satisfy their brutal revenge, bit off his flesh with their teeth. Thinking they had entirely deprived him of life, they cast him out into the fields.

But he miraculously recovered and returned publicly into the city. By patience and other miracles he wrought among them, many were converted from the error of their ways, and converted to become disciples of Jesus.

Departing from Sinope, he returned to Jerusalem. But he did not continue long in his native country, returning again to the province allotted him for the exercise of his ministry. It greatly flourished through the power of divine grace that attended it. He traveled over Thrace (now in Bulgaria, Greece, and Turkey), Macedonia (country of north Greece), Thessaly (region in east Greece), Achaia (Greece), and Epirus (region of west Greece), preaching the gospel, propagating Christianity, then confirming the doctrine he taught with signs and miracles.

At last, he came to Petrae, a city of Achaia, where he gave his last and greatest testimony to the gospel of his divine Master, sealing it with his blood. Aegenas, proconsul of Achaia, came at this time to Petrae. He observed that multitudes had abandoned the heathen religion and embraced the gospel of Christ. He had recourse to every method, both of favor and cruelty, to reduce the people to their old idolatry.

The Apostle, whom no difficulties or dangers could deter from performing the duties of his ministry, addressed himself to the proconsul. Andrew calmly put him in mind that, being only a judge of man, he ought to revere Him who was the supreme and impartial Judge of all. We must pay Him the divine honors due to His exalted majesty and abandon the impieties of his idolatrous worship.

Andrew further observed that if he would renounce his idolatries and heartily embrace the Christian faith, he could, with him and with the members of the Church, receive eternal happiness in the Messiah's kingdom.

The proconsul answered that he himself could never embrace this religion. He desired that those whom Andrew had everywhere seduced might be brought back to the ancient religion they had forsaken.

The Apostle replied that he saw it was in vain to endeavor to persuade a person incapable of sober counsels and hardened in his own blindness and folly. With regard to himself, he might act as he pleased. If the proconsul had any torment greater than another, he might heap that upon him. The greater constancy Andrew showed in his sufferings for Christ, the more acceptable he should be to his Lord and Master.

Aegnas could hold his rage no longer. After treating him with very offensive language and showing Andrew the most distinguished marks of contempt, he passed sentence upon him that he should be put to death. He first ordered him to be scourged, seven attendants successively whipping his naked body. Seeing the Apostle's invincible patience and constancy, he then commanded Andrew to be crucified by being fastened to the cross with cords instead of nails, that his death might be more lingering and tedious.

As Andrew was led to the place of his execution walking with a cheerful and composed mind, the people cried out that a good and innocent man was unjustly condemned to die.

On his coming near the cross, he saluted it in the following manner: "I have long desired and expected this happy hour. The cross has been consecrated by the body of Christ hanging on it, and adorned with His members as with so many inestimable jewels. I, therefore, come joyfully and triumphing to it, that it may receive me as a disciple and follower of Him who once hung upon it, and be the means of carrying me safe to my Master, being the instrument on which He redeemed me."

After offering up his prayers to the throne of grace, exhorting the people to constancy and perseverance in the faith he had delivered to them, he was fastened to the cross. He hung two whole days, teaching and instructing the people.

In the meantime, great interest was made to the proconsul to spare his life. However, the Apostle earnestly begged of the Almighty that he might now depart and seal the truth of his religion with his blood (see Hebrews 9:16-17). His prayers were heard. He died, it is said, on the last day of November, but of what year is uncertain.

His last prayer, uttered on that now sacred cross, ends this book, its words distilling reverential epitaphs for not just this one Apostle but in behalf of all of them.

There seems to have been something peculiar to the form of the cross on which he suffered. It is commonly thought to have been a cross-decussate, or two pieces of timber crossing each other in the center, in the form of the letter X and hence usually known by the name of St. Andrew's Cross.

His body being taken down from the cross, was decently and honorable interred by Maximillia, a lady of great quality and estate. She, Nicephorus (patriarch of Constantinople, lived A.D. 758–829) tells us, was wife to the same proconsul who crucified him.

Constantine the Great (c. A.D. 274–337) afterward removed his body to Constantinople and buried it in the great church he had built to the honor of the Apostles. In order to rebuild it, this structure was taken down some hundred years after by Justinian the Emperor (A.D. 483–565). The body of Andrew was found in a wooden coffin, and again deposited in its proper place in Constantinople (now Istanbul).

# Philip

*Philip findeth Nathanael, and saith unto him, We have found him, of whom Moses in the law, and the prophets, did write, Jesus of Nazareth, the son of Joseph.*

—John 1:45

# PHILIP

This Apostle was a native of Bethsaida, the city of the brothers, Andrew and Peter. His parentage, however, is unknown. He had the honor of being the first to be called to be an Apostle of the great Messiah.

Our Savior, soon after His return from the wilderness where He had been tempted by the devil, met with Andrew and his brother Peter, and after some discourse parted from them.

The next day, as Jesus was passing through Galilee, he found Philip, whom He presently commanded to follow Him. So the prerogative of being first called evidently belongs to Philip, he being the first of the Lord's Apostles. Though Andrew and Peter were the first that came and conversed with the Savior, yet they immediately returned to their occupation and were not called till a year after.

It cannot be doubted, that notwithstanding Philip was a native of Galilee, yet he was excellently skilled in the Law and the Prophets. Metaphrastes (ca. A.D. 950–1000) assures us that he had, from his childhood, been excellently educated. He frequently read over the books of Moses and attentively considered the prophecies relating to the coming of the Messiah.

Nor was our Apostle idle after the honor he had received of being called to attend the Savior. He immediately imparted the glad tidings of the Messiah's appearance to his friend Nathanael Bartholomew and conducted him to his Savior.

After his being called to be an Apostle, we have very little recorded of him by the evangelists. It was, however, to him that our Savior proposed the question as to where they should find bread sufficient to satisfy the hunger of so great a multitude. Philip answered, that it was not easy to procure so great a quantity, not considering that it was equally easy for Almighty Power to feed multitudes when it should be His divine will.

It was also to the same Apostle that the Gentile proselytes, who came up to worship at Jerusalem, applied, when they were desirous to see the Savior. And it was with him our Lord had the discourse a little before the Paschal Supper, recorded by John.

Jesus had been fortifying their minds with proper considerations against His departure from them. He had told them that He was going to prepare for them a place in the mansions of the heavenly Canaan. He was "the way, the truth, and the life; that no man could come to the Father but by Him."

Philip, not thoroughly understanding the force of his Master's reasoning, begged of Him that He would show them the Father.

Our Lord gently reproved his ignorance, that after attending so long to His instructions, he should not know that He was the image of the Father. He is the express character of His infinite wisdom, power, and goodness appearing in Him. He said and did nothing but by His Father's appointment, which if they did not believe, His miracles were a sufficient evidence. Such demands were, therefore, unnecessary and impertinent.

Demanding any sign was an indication of great weakness in him, after three years' education under His discipline and instruction, to appear so ignorant with regard to these particulars.

The ancients tell us that in the distribution made by the Apostles of the several regions of the world, Upper Asia fell to Philip's share where he labored with an indefatigable diligence and industry, attended by his sister, Mariamne. (Sadly, she was never referred to in New Testament text and, therefore, is not listed in Women and the Work, a chart after the endnotes in this book.) By the constancy and power of his preaching, and the efficacy of his miracles, he gained numerous converts whom he baptized into the Christian faith.

Philip also cured at once their bodies of infirmities and distempers, and their souls of errors and idolatry. He continued with them a considerable time in settling churches and appointing them guides and ministers of religion.

After several years successfully exercising his apostolical office in all those parts, he came at last to Hierapolis, in Phrygia (southwest Asia Minor), a city remarkably rich and populous, but at the same time overrun with the most enormous idolatry.

Philip, being grieved to see the people so wretchedly enslaved by error and superstition, continually offered his address to heaven. By his prayers and often calling on the name of Christ, he procured the death, or, at least, the vanishing of an enormous serpent to which they paid adoration.

Having thus demolished their deity, he demonstrated to them how ridiculous and unjust it was for them to pay divine honors to such horrible creatures. He showed them that God alone was to be worshiped as the great Parent of all the world, who, in the beginning, made man after His glorious image.

When mankind became fallen from that innocent and happy state, God sent His own Son into the world to redeem them. In order to perform this glorious work, He died on the cross, and rose again from the dead. At the end of the world, Jesus will come again to raise all the sons of men from the chambers of the dust and sentence them to everlasting rewards and punishments.

This discourse roused them from their lethargy. They were ashamed of their late idolatry, and great numbers embraced the doctrines of the gospel.

This provoked the great enemy of mankind, and he had recourse to his old methods—cruelty and persecution. The magistrates of the city seized the Apostle. After having thrown him into prison, they caused him to be scourged. When this preparatory cruelty was over, he was led to execution. Being bound, he was hanged against a pillar; or, according to others, crucified.

The Apostle being dead, his body was taken down by Nathanael Bartholomew, his fellow laborer in the gospel, and Mariamne, Philip's sister, the constant companion of his travels. After he was decently buried, they confirmed the people in the faith of Christ and departed from them.

# Nathanael Bartholomew

*Nathanael answered and saith unto him, Rabbi, thou art the Son of God; thou art the King of Israel. And he saith unto him, Verily, verily, I say unto you, Hereafter ye shall see heaven open, and the angels of God ascending and descending upon the Son of man.*

—John 1:49, 51

# NATHANAEL BARTHOLOMEW

I n respect to this Apostle, there occurs a primary question about his name, which is given so differently in different sacred authorities, as to induce a strong suspicion that the two names refer to two totally distinct persons.

The reasons for applying these words, Nathanael and Bartholomew, to the same person, are these circumstances:

1. None of the three first evangelists mention any person named Nathanael.

2. John never mentions the name Bartholomew.

3. Bartholomew is mentioned by the three first evangelists, on all the lists, directly after Philip, who is by John represented as his intimate friend.

4. Bartholomew is not an individual name, but a word showing parentage merely, the first syllable being often prefixed to Syriac names, for this purpose. *Bar*-Tholomew means the "son of Tholomew," "Tholomai," or "Tolmai," just as Bar-Jonah means

the "son of Jonah." The former was not any more in reality the personal, individual name of Nathanael, than the latter was of Peter; but some circumstance may have occurred to make it, in this instance, often take the place of the true individual name.

A few very brief notices are given of this Apostle by John, who alone alludes to him, other than a bare mention on the lists. It is mentioned in his Gospel that Nathanael was of Cana, in Galilee, a town which stood about halfway between lake of Gennesaret (Sea of Galilee) and the Mediterranean Sea.

The circumstances of his call seem to show that he was then with Philip, probably at or near Bethsaida. Philip, after being summoned by Jesus to the apostleship, immediately sought to bring his friend Nathanael into an enjoyment of the honors of a personal association with Jesus. He sought him out and invited him to become a follower of the Messiah, foretold by Moses and the prophets who had now appeared as Jesus of Nazareth.

On hearing of that mean place as the home of the promised King of Israel, Nathanael, with great scorn, replied, in inquiry, "Can any good thing come out of Nazareth?"

To this sneering question, Philip answered by the simple proposition, "Come and see"—wisely judging that no argument could answer his friend's prejudice so well as an actual observation of the character and aspect of the Nazarene himself. [15]

Nathanael, accordingly, persuaded by the earnestness of his friend, went along with him, perhaps, partly to gratify him. Probably his curiosity was somewhat moved to know what could have thus brought Philip into this devout regard for a citizen of that dirty little town. He readily accompanied Philip to see what sort of prophet could come out of Nazareth.

The words with which Jesus greeted Nathanael, even before he had been personally introduced or was prepared for any salutation, are the most exalted testimonial of his character that could be conceived. Jesus voiced at once his very eminent qualifications for the high honors of the apostleship.

When Jesus saw Nathanael coming to Him, He said, "Behold a true son of Israel, in whom there is no guile!"— manifesting at once a confidential and intimate knowledge of his whole character. Nathanael, quite surprised at this remarkable compliment from one whom he had never seen until that moment and whom he supposed to be equally ignorant of him, replied with the inquiry, "Whence knowest thou me?"

Jesus answered, "Before Philip called thee, when thou was under the fig tree, I saw thee."

The fig trees of Palestine, presenting a wide leafy cover and a delightful shade, were often used in the warm season as places of retirement. Whether in company, for conversation, or in solitude, for meditation and prayer, it was, doubtless, in one of these occupations that Nathanael was engaged.

The eye that could pierce the stormy shades of night on the boisterous waves of Galilee, that could search the hearts of men, could also penetrate the thick, leafy veil of the fig tree. Jesus could observe the most secret actions of this guileless Israelite, when Nathanael supposed the whole world to be shut out and gave himself to the undisguised enjoyment of his thoughts, feeling, and actions without restraint.

Nathanael, struck with sudden but absolute conviction at this amazing display of knowledge, gave up all his proud scruples against the Nazarene, and adoringly exclaimed, "Rabbi! Thou art the Son of God; Thou art the King of Israel."

Jesus, recognizing with pleasure the ready faith of this pure-minded Apostle, replied, "Because I said unto thee, 'I saw thee under the fig tree,' believest thou? Thou shalt yet see greater things than these."

Then turning to Philip as well as to Nathanael, He said to them both, "I solemnly assure you, hereafter ye shall see heaven open, and the angels of God ascending and descending upon the Son of Man."

The next day after this occurrence, as John records, Jesus was in Cana of Galilee, the hometown of Nathanael and was present at a wedding that took place there. From the circumstance that the mother of Jesus was there also, it would seem likely that it was the marriage of some of their family friends. This conjecture might seem allowable, that the presence of Jesus and His Apostles on this occasion was in some way connected with the introduction of

Nathanael to Jesus. Perhaps this new Apostle may have been in some way concerned in this interesting event.

It is probable therefore, that Jesus accompanied Nathanael home from Bethsaida, or whatever place was the scene of his calling to the apostleship, along with Philip.

After this first incident, no mention whatever is made of Nathanael, either under his proper name, or his paternal appellation, except that when the Twelve were sent forth in pairs, he was sent together with his friend Philip. Those who had been summoned to work together might now go forth laboring together in this high commission.

Another incident is also told by John, in which Nathanael is concerned, namely, the meeting on the lake of Gennesaret after the Resurrection. His name is mentioned among those who went out on the fishing excursion with Peter. His friend Philip is not mentioned, but may have been one of the "two disciples," who are included without their names being given.

From this trifling circumstance, some have concluded that Nathanael was a fisherman by trade, as well as the other four who are mentioned with him. The conjecture is improbable, as his residence was at Cana, which is commonly understood to have been an inland town. Other idle conjectures about his occupation and rank might be guessed at, but let the dust of ages sleep on the guesses of the Gregories, of Chrysostom, Augustin, and their reverential copyists in modern times.

There is a dim relic of a story, of quite ancient date, that after the dispersion of the Apostles, he went to India, northwestern Africa, Armenia, and Arabia and preached there till his death. This is highly probable.

It is well known that many of the Jews, more particularly after the destruction of Jerusalem, settled along the coasts of the Red Sea where they continued for centuries. It is reasonable to suppose that after the wasting fury of invasion had desolated the city and land of their fathers, many of the Christian Jews went forth to seek a new home in the peaceful regions of Arabia Felix (south Arabia, close to modern Yemen) and other countries close by.

With them also went forth this true Israelite without guile, to devote the rest of his life to apostolic labors in that distant country. Those of his wandering brethren who had believed in Christ, would so much need the support and counsel of one of the divinely commissioned ministers of the gospel. Those Israelites, too, who still continued as unbelievers, would present objects of importance in the view of the Apostle.

All the visible glories of the ancient covenant had departed. In that distant land, with so little of the chilling influence of the dogmatical teachers of the law round them, they would be more readily led to the just appreciation of a spiritual faith and in a simple creed of Christianity.

It seems that Nathanael met his end in Armenia at Albana, which is modern Derbend. The story runs as follows, quoting from *The Apostolic History* of Abdias:

Bartholomew preached with such success that the heathen gods were rendered powerless. A very interesting personal description of him is given. "He has black, curly hair, white skin, large eyes, straight nose, his hair covers his eyes, his beard long and grizzled, middle height. He wears a white robe with a purple stripe, and a white cloak with four purple gems at the corners. For twenty-six years has he worn these, and they never grow old. His shoes have lasted twenty-six years. He prays a hundred times a day and a hundred times at night. His voice is like a trumpet; angels wait upon him; he is always cheerful and knows all languages."

Bartholomew did many wonderful things there, including the healing of the lunatic daughter of the king, the exposing of the king's idol and the banishing of the demon who inhabited it. The demon was visibly banished from the idol by an angel, and there is an interesting description of that demon—"black, sharp-faced, with a long beard, hair to the feet, fiery eyes, breathing flame and spiky wings like a hedge-hog."

The king and many others were baptized; but the priests remained hostile. The priests went to the king's brother, Astyages. The king's brother had Bartholomew arrested, beaten with clubs, flayed alive and crucified in agony. And so Nathanael Bartholomew died a martyr for his Lord.

The traditional founders of the Armenian Church were the Apostles Thaddeus and Bartholomew, whose tombs are shown and venerated in Armenia as sacred shrines. [*Treasures of the Armenian Patriarchate of Jerusalem,* Arpag Mekhitarian, Helen and Edward Mardigian Musem–Catalog no. 1 Jerusalem, Armenian Patriarchate, 1969.]

# The Triumphs of the Twelve

According to *A Traveller's Guide to Saints in Europe,* "A written account says that after the Emperor Anastasius built the City of Duras in Mesopotamia in 508, he caused the relics [Nathanael's remains] to be taken there. Gregory of Tours assures us that, before the end of the sixth century, they were carried to the Lipari Islands near Sicily; and Anastasius, the Librarian, tells us that in 809 they were taken to Benevento and then transported to Rome in 983 by the Emperor Otto III. They now lie in the Church of St. Bartholomew-on-Tiber in a porphyry shrine under the high altar. An arm was sent by the Bishop of Benevento to St. Edward the Confessor of Britain, who gave it to Canterbury Cathedral."

# Thomas Didymus

*Then said Thomas, which is called Didymus, unto his*
*fellowdisciples, Let us also go, that we may die with him.*
—John 11:16

# THOMAS DIDYMUS

he second name of this Apostle is only the Greek translation of the former, which is the Syriac and Hebrew word for a "twin brother." *One* important circumstance may be safely inferred about the *birth* of Thomas. Beyond this, antiquity bears no record whatever of his circumstances previous to his admission into the apostolic fraternity.

Nor is the authentic history of the Apostles much more satisfactory in respect to subsequent parts of Thomas' history. A very few brief but striking incidents in which he was involved are specified by John alone.

John seems to have been disposed to supply some characteristic account of several of the Apostles who had been noticed only by name in the writings of Matthew, Mark, and Luke.

Those in particular who received this peculiar notice from him are Andrew, Philip, Nathanael, Thomas, and John himself. All, as well as Peter, have some interesting matters, which, though trivial, do much towards giving a distinct impression of some of the leading traits in their characters. Among these facts respecting Thomas, however, there is not one that gives us any account of his parentage, rank in life, or previous occupation. No other authentic sources bring any more facts to view on these points.

The only conclusion presented even by conjecture about his early history, is, that he was a publican, like Matthew. This notion is grounded, no doubt, on the circumstance that in all the gospel lists, he is paired with Matthew—as though there were some close connection between them. This is only a conjecture.

Of the three incidents commemorated by John, two are such as to present Thomas in a light by no means advantageous to his character as a ready and earnest believer in Jesus. On both these occasions he is represented as expressing opinions which prove him to have been very slow, not only in believing, but also in comprehending spiritual truths.

The first incident is that mentioned by John in his account of the death of Lazarus. He describes the effect produced on the Apostles by the news of the decease of their friend. Jesus intends to go to Judea again, in spite of all the mortal dangers to which He was there exposed. The Jews are enraged at His open declaration of His divine character and origin. Many have vowed to punish with death One who advanced claims which they pronounced absolutely blasphemous.

This mortal hatred is so openly expressed that Jesus Himself had thought it best to retire awhile from that region. Even He tried to avoid exposing Himself to the fatal effects of such malice until the other great duties of His earthly mission had been executed. Only then could He proceed to the bloody fulfillment of His mighty task with the assurance that He had finished the work that His Father gave Him to do.

But in spite of the pressing opposition by His Apostles, Jesus expressed His firm resolution to go. Thomas found his Master determined to rush into the danger, which, by once retiring from it for a time, He had acknowledged to be imminent. Turning to his fellow Apostles, he said, "Let us also go, that we may die with him."

The proposal, thus decidedly made, shows a noble resolution in Thomas. He wanted to share all the fortunes of Him to whom he had joined himself, and it presents his character in a far more favorable light than the other passages in which his conduct is revealed.

While the rest feared the peril of the journey, Thomas boldly proposed to his companions to follow unhesitatingly in the footsteps of their Master, whithersoever He might go, thus evincing a spirit of far more exalted devotion to the cause.

In John's minute account of the parting discourses of Christ at the Last Supper, Jesus spoke of His departure as very near. In order to comfort His Apostles, He told them He was going "to prepare a place for them, in His Father's house, where there were many mansions." Assuring them of His speedy return to bring them to these mansions of rest, He said to them, "Whither I go ye know and the way ye know."

Yet so lost, for the time, were all these words of instruction and counsel that not one of His followers seems to have rightly apprehended the force of this remark. Thomas was probably only expressing the general doubt when he replied to Jesus, in much perplexity at the language, "Lord, we know not whither Thou goest; and how can we know the way?"

Jesus replied, "I am the way, the truth, and the life; no man comes to the Father but by Me." But equally vain was this new illustration of the truth.

The remark that Philip next made, begging that they might have their curiosity gratified by a sight of the Father, shows how earnestly they were all still dreaming of a worldly, tangible, and visible kingdom. They mistook all the plain declarations of Jesus for their own preconceived, deep-rooted notions.

Nor was this optimistic error removed till the descent of that Holy Spirit of Truth which their long-suffering and ever watchful Lord invoked. It taught their still darkened souls the things that they would not now see. It brought to their remembrance all that they now so little heeded.

After the Apostles had seen their great Master expired on the cross, their minds were distracted by the hopes and fears concerning His Resurrection, about which they were not then fully satisfied. Perhaps this engaged Him the sooner to hasten His appearances, that by the sensible manifestations of Himself He might put the matter beyond all possibility of dispute. Accordingly, the very day in which He arose from the dead, He came into the house where they were assembled, while, for fear of the Jews, the doors about them were closed shut. He gave them sufficient assurance that He was risen from the dead.

At this meeting, Thomas was absent, having probably never rejoined their company since their dispersion in the garden as everyone's fears prompted him to look after his own safety. At his return, they told him that the Lord had appeared to them. He obstinately refused to give credit to what they said or to believe that it was really He.[16] Rather, he presumed they saw a specter, or an apparition, unless he might see the very print of the nails and feel the wounds in His hands and side.

Our Savior would not take the least notice of his perverse obstinacy. After seven days, at night He came again to them as they were solemnly met to perform their devotions. Calling to Thomas, Jesus bade him look upon His hands, put his fingers into the print of the nails, and thrust his hand into His side, to satisfy his faith by a demonstration from the senses.

Thomas was soon convinced of his error and obstinacy, confessing that he now acknowledged Him to be his Lord and Master, saying, "My Lord and my God."

Our Lord answered that it was happy for him that he believed the testimony of his own senses; but that it would have been more commendable in him to have believed without seeing. It was foretold that the Son of God should burst the chains of death and rise again from the dead.

Our great Redeemer, according to the promise before His Ascension, poured an extraordinary effusion of the Holy Ghost upon the Apostles to qualify them for the great work of preaching the gospel. Thomas, as well as the rest, preached the gospel in several parts of Judea. After the dispersion of the Christian Church in Jerusalem, he repaired into Parthia (once Persia and is now called Iran), the province assigned him for his ministry.

After which, as Sempronius and others inform us, he preached the gospel to the Medes (now northwest Iran), Persians (modern Iran), Carminians, Hyrcani (part of Persia, southeast of Caspian Sea), Bactrians (west Asia, between Oxus River and Hindu Kush Mountains), and the neighboring nations.

During his preaching in Persia, Thomas is said to have met with the magi, or wise men, who had taken that long journey at our Savior's birth to worship Him. He baptized them and took them with him as his companions and assistants in propagating the gospel. How merciful is our God to answer the prayers of the pure in heart who wait on Him.

Leaving Persia, he traveled into Ethiopia (northeast Africa, bordering Egypt and the Red Sea), preaching the glad tidings of the gospel. He healed their sick and worked other miracles to prove he had his commission from on high. After traveling through these countries, he entered India.

When the Portuguese first visited these countries, after their discovery of a passage by the Cape of Good

Hope, they received the following particulars, preserved by the Christians in these parts: Thomas came first to Socotora, an island in the Arabian Sea, and thence to Cranganor, where he converted many from the error of their ways. He traveled further into the East. Then, having successfully preached the gospel, returned back to the kingdom of Coromandel (southeast India).

At Meliapur, the metropolis of the kingdom, not far from the mouth of the Ganges, he began to erect a place for divine worship. It was prohibited by the idolatrous priests and Sagamo, prince of that country. But after performing several miracles, the work was suffered to proceed. Sagamo himself embraced the Christian faith, whose example was soon followed by great numbers of his friends and subjects.

This remarkable success alarmed the Brahmins, who plainly perceived that their religion would soon be extirpated unless some method could be found for putting a stop to the progress of Christianity. They therefore resolved to put the Apostle to death.

At a small distance from the city was a tomb, whither Thomas often retired for private devotion. Hither the Brahmins and their armed followers pursued him. While he was at prayer, they first shot at him a shower of darts, after which one of the priests ran him through with a lance.

His body was taken up by his disciples and buried in the church he had lately erected. It was afterwards improved into a structure of great magnificence.

Chrysostom (patriarch of Constantinople, A.D. 349 –407) says that Thomas was at first the weakest and most incredulous of all the Apostles. He learned, through Christ's condescending, to satisfy his doubts, and with the power of Divine grace, became the most active and invincible of them all. He traveled over most parts of the world. He lived without fear in the midst of barbarous nations.

# Judas Iscariot

*Then Judas, which had betrayed him, when he saw that he [Jesus] was condemned, repented . . . Saying, I have sinned in that I have betrayed the innocent blood.*

—Matthew 27:3–4

# JUDAS ISCARIOT

"**I**scariot" means a man of Carioth or Kerioth, a city of Judah (Joshua 15:25), toward the coast of Edom southward. The traitor was the only representative of Judea in the college of Apostles, as all the others were Galileans.

We know nothing about his early days, though his father's name, Simon, is given. But to search the scriptures for this particular Simon will be vain. He is known only by the misfortune of having such a son. The apocryphal Gospels narrate many stories concerning him, but of course, no credit is to be given them.

He is first brought to our notice in that chapter of John's Gospel where the Savior delivers the sermon upon the Bread of Life. It was just after He had performed the great miracle of feeding the multitude. The words of Jesus were misunderstood by some who stood by and proved a stumbling block to them.

"There are some of you that believe not," said the Savior. To these words, the evangelist adds his own comment: "Jesus knew from the beginning who they were that believed not, and who he was that should betray Him."

We might say that the faith of all the Apostles was weak and wavering at first. They all seemed to have some little difficulty in appreciating the spirituality of the Lord's words. But His eye had detected one among them who was covetous and disloyal and in whose heart the seeds of treachery were just beginning to germinate.

Shortly after, Jesus says in reply to Peter's noble confession, "Have I not chosen you Twelve, and one of you is a devil?" John adds another comment, "He spoke of Judas Iscariot, the son of Simon, for he it was that should betray Him, being one of the Twelve."

There is no proof that Judas thus early had conceived the idea of betraying Christ or that at some time he felt himself shunned by the rest of the Apostles. Some have supposed that he did really know himself to be the devil referred to by Christ, that his nature was so corrupt and callous that no moral pang troubled his conscience. But evil such as his is usually a plant of slow growth. "No one," says the old proverb, "becomes extremely wicked all of a sudden."

It is more in accordance with average human nature to look upon Judas Iscariot as a man who had begun well, but, without any fixed principles of right, was blown about by every chance wind. He was a man of strong passions and ungoverned impulses, one who could be very good or very bad.

Probably at this early stage, no dream of treason had suggested itself to him—nor had his fellow Apostles conscious suspicion of his inward character. Up to the very night of the betrayal, no one of them knew who should deliver up the Master. Nothing had hitherto happened which should make them suspect Judas particularly.

Yet, though the evil which was latent in the heart of the fallen Apostle was unperceived by his companions and himself, we cannot evade the fact that Jesus foresaw the end. This being so, the question very easily arises, "Why did the Savior admit to His confidence one who should betray Him?"

The most reasonable supposition is, that Jesus possibly discerned in Judas Iscariot qualities of heart and mind which would make him, under proper training, a useful man to advance the Master's cause. Jesus yearned over him with a tender love, striving to win him to Himself, but soon discovered that evil was far more powerful in him than good.

Just as the same sun that shines on the wax and melts it will shine on the clay and harden it, the difference is not in the sun that shines, but in the material upon which its beams fall. So the heart of Judas Iscariot, like that of Pharaoh, became less and less susceptible to the Savior's melting kindness. By and by, Jesus warns him, gives him liberty to depart, and finally sends him away with dignity to await calmly the treachery of perdition.

It is unquestionably a very difficult problem how to reconcile the divine foreknowledge of Jesus and the human freedom of Judas. We must admit both facts and await God's time for their reconciliation.

If the disposition of Judas Iscariot was bad, it may

reasonably be supposed that the badness would show itself upon provocation. In John's Gospel, we have a scene presented to us that plainly shows what the peculiar vice of this Apostle was. Jesus was on a visit to Bethany, where He had raised Lazarus from the dead, and while there, a supper was made for Him.

During the entertainment, we are told, "then took Mary a pound of ointment of spikenard, very costly, and anointed the feet of Jesus and wiped His feet with her hair, and the house was filled with the odor of the ointment." It was a delicate, loving compliment to our Lord, very graceful and generous. As such, it could have met with nothing but approval from every right-hearted man. After all, Jesus had just restored her brother to life, a priceless gift!

But how does it affect Judas? "Then, saith one of His disciples, Judas Iscariot, Simon's son, who was to betray Him, 'Why was not this ointment sold for three hundred pence and given to the poor?'" From any man with the slightest feeling of decency and propriety, the suggestion would have seemed a petty one. But coming from one who was supposed to have loved his Lord, it was cold and heartless.

But in Judas Iscariot all feelings of propriety, all emotions of love, were crushed by the hand of his master passion, greed. We are told the reason for his hypocritical remark by the historian: "Not that he cared for the poor, but because he was a thief, and had the bag, and bore what was put therein."

Thus it is apparent that the love of money, which love is the root of all evil, exercised a powerful sway over this unhappy man. He was the steward of the company. His opportunities were favorable, his passion was strong, but his principles were weak. Thus, his comrades as well as the poor suffered by him. How mean and low is the character thus presented to us!

We need not care to ask with what motives he had joined himself to the apostolic company. It seems scarcely possible that any prospect of gain could have presented itself at first. We see him now as he has become; to what depth his inordinate desire for gain has reduced him!

It is more than possible that he was appointed to take care of the funds because some peculiar capacity for business may have been discovered in him. Maybe it was a test applied by his Master, a sort of touchstone to bring out the real character of the man.

Smarting under the reproof that his Master had given him at the anointing and angered at the loss of the three hundred pence that might have been his, Judas Iscariot steals away in a rage that night from Bethany. He goes up to Jerusalem, seeks a private interview with the priests, and asks, "How much are you willing to give me, and I will betray Jesus unto you?"

How long they bargained, how much they beat the traitor down in price, we are left to imagine. We learn only the sum offered and accepted for which Judas was to deliver up his Master and consign himself to everlasting ignominy. Thirty pieces of silver is between fifteen and twenty dollars, the ransom money of the meanest slave!

And now the night of the Last Supper has come. The Apostles and the Savior are gathered about the board, the blessed memorials of His death and sacrifice have been partaken of. Jesus, rising from His couch, proceeds to wash the feet of the Apostles, even those of the traitor himself. Surely, may He not have taken this opportunity to whisper a last word of warning? Warning, indeed, does come in the words, "Ye are clean, but not all."

The towel is laid aside, the reclining posture resumed, and then Jesus says, "I speak not of you all; I know whom I have chosen; but that the scripture may be fulfilled, he that eateth bread with me hath lifted his heel against me." How touching and melancholy these words sound! They are words of deep, divine, omniscient, patient, long-forbearing love. How hard must that heart have been that could withstand them!

At last, the pent-up secret which troubled the Master was set free by the exclamation, "Verily, verily I say unto you, that one of you shall betray me." The Apostles receive this announcement with sad amazement. Exceedingly grieved, they look upon each other, and in conscious innocence ask Jesus, "Lord, is it I?"

Jesus, who had just before pointed out the traitor by a sign to Peter and John, answered, "He that dippeth his bread with me in the dish, the same shall betray me."

Judas Iscariot, who probably saw that his Master's hand and his own were together in the dish, and that consequently he was accused of the treason, thinks perhaps to brazen it out, feeling sure that his secret is guarded from the others. Yet he feels compelled to say something, and so asks the same question, "Lord, is it I?"

Jesus says directly, "Thou hast said," and then adds, "That which thou doest, do quickly."

Judas Iscariot, seeing that he is discovered, goes immediately out. "And it was night," adds the evangelist. The sentence is short, but what a meaning is wrapped up in it! It was night indeed. Over the soul of Judas Iscariot, such a pall of awful darkness fell that the light of morning never rose upon it again (Matthew 27:3–10).

And now the small company, relieved of the traitor's presence, sang a hymn together and then went forth into the Garden of Gethsemane. The Savior passed through that agony which no eye beheld. As He awakened His sleeping Apostles, He is met by Judas Iscariot and his armed band. The kiss of betrayal is given; the design of Judas Iscariot is at last accomplished. The Lord of Life is yielded up to death.

The Apostles all forsake their Master, as He had foretold, while Judas Iscariot, slinking away through the trees of the garden, goes to the city to receive the reward of his treachery.

Is he happy now that he has reached what he was striving for? At first, perhaps, he is. But the gratification is only for a moment. The time for reflection has come. The betrayer has heard the sentence of death pronounced upon his victim. He recalls the many hours they have passed together in sweet communion. He remembers how good his Master always was to him, and how pure a life was that which is doomed to death. Remorse, coupled with despair, takes hold upon him.

Seeing that Jesus was condemned, the narrative tells us he "repented himself, and brought again the thirty pieces of silver to the chief priests and elders, saying, I have sinned, in that I have betrayed the innocent blood." That cry was not the cry simply of rage or mortification, but a plain admission that he had done wickedly. What a testimony it is to the pure life of Jesus! Judas Iscariot, His only betrayer, leaves no court testimony against Jesus Christ!

It would have been for the interest of Judas Iscariot to persuade himself, if he possibly could, that his Master had done something unworthy. Rather he is forced to confess, like Pilate, "I find no fault in him." Such a confession from the intimate enemy of Jesus speaks volumes.

In returning the money, he may have had a dim hope that it would be taken back and his Lord released, but this hope is crushed by the words of the priests; "What is that to us? See thou to that."

Thus are the emissaries of Satan rewarded. He uses them to complete his purposes. They sacrifice honor, self-respect, strength, and then are flung away to die in shame. Thus the hard heart of Judas Iscariot dies. The answer of the priests comes with stunning force upon his heart.

All hope of saving Jesus is taken from him. His crime must work out to the bitter end. He cannot bear the thought of life, with the pale face of his Victim ever looking reproachfully upon him. Conscience stings him like the serpents of the Furies. To escape from himself, he turns, flings down the filthy lucre, the price of blood, upon the pavement, and goes and hangs himself.

At the southern end of the long ridge of Olivet, on the top of the Hill of Evil Counsel, there is a single wind-driven, storm-scarred tree, called the Tree of Judas, from the branches of which tradition says the traitor hung himself. The manner of his death is not precisely stated, though we get the clearest account in the first chapter of The Acts. It may be that while he was attempting to commit suicide the rope broke under the shock of his falling weight and so his bowels gushed out.

One writer says that the account of The Acts does not refer to the manner of his death, but to the way in which his corpse was treated after death, according to the Jewish custom of treating suicides.

And here we leave him, pity struggling with indignation as we read his awful history. He is truly a man of whom it has been said that it would have been better for him if he had not been born.

# Matthias

*Go ye therefore, and teach all nations, baptizing them
in the name of the Father, and of the Son, and of the Holy
Ghost: Teaching them to observe all things whatsoever I have
commanded you: and, lo, I am with you alway, [even] unto
the end of the world. Amen.*

—Matthew 28:19–20

# Matthias

Matthias was not an Apostle of the first election, immediately called and chosen by the Son of God himself. He was one of our Lord's disciples, probably one of the Seventy, who had attended Him during the time of His public ministry.

The defection of Judas Iscariot having made a vacancy in the family of Apostles, the first thing they did after their return from Mount Olivet, when their great Master ascended to the throne of glory, was to fill up this vacancy with a proper person.

Accordingly, two persons were proposed. Joseph, called Barsabas, and Matthias, both duly qualified for this important office. The method of election was by lots, a way common both by Jews and Gentiles for determining doubtful and difficult cases, especially in choosing judges or magistrates.

This course seems to have been taken by the Apostles because the Holy Ghost was not yet fully given, by whose immediate dictates and inspirations they were afterwards chiefly guided. The prayer being ended the lots were drawn, by which it appeared that Matthias was the person. He was accordingly numbered among the Twelve Apostles.

Not long after this election, the promised powers of the Holy Ghost were conferred upon the Apostles to qualify them for that great and difficult employment upon which they were sent, namely, the establishing of the holy religion of the Son of God among the children of men. Matthias' election to his apostleship with the other eleven was guided by group prayer to God, and then validated by the Holy Ghost.

Our Apostle remained, after his appointment, for about a year in the neighborhood of Jerusalem, and preached in various parts of Judea, his native country. When persecution arose, he was obliged to leave this devoted capital, soon to be destroyed.

The particular scene of his labor, though not certainly ascertained, is believed to have been first in Macedonia. Here, it is said, the Gentiles tried his faith and integrity by giving him a poisonous and intoxicating potion that he unhesitatingly drank in the name of Christ—without the least harm to himself. When a similar potion had deprived more than two hundred and fifty of their sight, he, laying his hands upon them, restored their vision.

Nicephorus says that our Apostle traveled eastward and remained for some time in Cappadocia (mistakenly called Ethiopia by Nicephorus). His residence at this time was near the eruption of the river Apsarus, and the haven Hyssus, both places in Cappadocia.

This district was at that period in a very barbarous state. Its inhabitants, in consequence, treated the Apostle with great rudeness and inhumanity. After all his labors and sufferings, and a numerous conversion of men to Christianity, he obtained at last the crown of martyrdom in A.D. 61 or 64.

It is uncertain by what kind of death he left the regions of mortality and sealed the truth of the gospel he had so assiduously preached with his blood. Dorotheus (bishop of Tyre, ca. A.D. 255–362) says he finished his course at Sebastopol (southwest Asia Minor), and was buried there near the Temple of the Sun in A.D. 64. An ancient martyrology reports him to have been seized by the Jews and as a blasphemer, to have been stoned and then beheaded. But, the Greek offices, supported herein by the authority of several ancient breviaries (books of daily prayers and readings), tell us that he was crucified.

There are at least two separate sites where his bones are supposedly buried. One is in Rome, Italy, and the other is in Trier, Germany, both reputedly transported there by Queen Helena (died A.D. 330), mother of Constantine the Great.

# Acts of the
# Apostles

# ACTS OF THE APOSTLES

| Date | Scripture | Occurrence |
|------|-----------|------------|
| A.D. 30 (Visits of Jesus after His Resurrection) | Acts 1:2–3 | Jesus was with his Apostles for 40 days after His Resurrection. |
| | Acts 1:4–8 | Christ's final instructions on Mount of Olives. |
| | Acts 1:9 | Ascension of Christ. |
| | Acts 1:10–11 | Christ will "so come in like manner as ye have seen him go into heaven." |
| | Acts 1:12:13 | Apostles return to the upper room. |
| | Acts 1:14 | Apostles pray with Mary and other women. |
| | Acts 1:15–22 | Peter talks to 120 disciples to replace Judas Iscariot. |
| | Acts 1:23–26 | Matthias chosen as an Apostle. |
| A.D. 30 (10 days after Jesus left) | Acts 2 | On the Day of Pentecost, the Holy Ghost fills everyone and they speak in tongues; 3120 are baptized to form first Church (in Jerusalem). |
| | Acts 3:1–11 | Peter and John heal lame man at the gate of temple. |

# Acts of the Apostles

| Date | Scripture | Occurrence |
|------|-----------|------------|
| A.D. 30 (10 days after Jesus left) (cont.) | Acts 3:12–26 | Peter preaches in the temple about Jesus. |
| | Acts 4:1–4 | Peter and John arrested, but 5000 believe. |
| | Acts 4:5–7 | Peter and John questioned by high priests. |
| | Acts 4:7–12 | Peter tells of his authority. |
| | Acts 4:13–18 | High priests and council warn Apostles not to preach in the name of Jesus. |
| | Acts 4:19–20 | Peter and John reply that they must speak of the things they have seen and heard. |
| | Acts 4:21–23 | Peter and John released, return, and report. |
| | Acts 4:24–30 | Apostles pray for boldness in speech. |
| | Acts 4:31 | Apostles' wish granted with Holy Ghost. |
| | Acts 4:32–35 | Church members hold all things in common and there is no poor among them. |
| | Acts 4:36–37 | Joses, a Levite, sells land and gives money. |
| | Acts 5:1–11 | Ananias and Sapphira hold back money and die. |
| | Acts 5:12–16 | Many signs and wonders done by Apostles. |
| | Acts 5:17–18 | High priest and Sadducees jail Apostles. |
| | Acts 5:19 | An angel opens prison doors. |

# The Triumphs of the Twelve

| Date | Scripture | Occurrence |
|------|-----------|------------|
| A.D. 30 (10 days after Jesus left) (cont.) | Acts 5:20–21 | Apostles told to preach at the temple. |
| | Acts 5:21–27 | Sanhedrin brings Apostles before them for preaching in the name of Jesus. |
| | Acts 5:27–33 | Peter's testimony of Christ's Resurrection. |
| | Acts 5:34–39 | Gamaliel, a Sanhedrin member, cautions council to leave the Apostles alone. |
| | Acts 5:40–42 | Sanhedrin commands Apostles not to preach in the name of Jesus again, and let them go. |
| | Acts 6:1 | A dispute arises between the Greek and Hebrew members, because the Greek widows were being neglected. |
| | Acts 6:2–4 | Apostles call disciples together to select seven helpers. |
| | Acts 6:5–6 | Seven men chosen and set apart by laying on of hands. |
| A.D. 30 | Acts 6:7 | Number of disciples in Jerusalem increases. |
| | Acts 8:1–8 | Church persecuted in Jerusalem. Members scattered. |
| | Acts 8:4 | Scattered members preach the gospel. |
| | Acts 8:5–8 | Philip was believed because people saw miracles. |
| | Acts 8:9–13 | Simon the sorcerer baptized by Philip. |

# Acts of the Apostles

| Date | Scripture | Occurrence |
|------|-----------|------------|
| A.D. 30 (cont.) | Acts 8:14–17 | Peter and John give the Holy Ghost to Philip's converts. |
| | Acts 8:11–24 | Simon wants to buy priesthood power but is rebuked. |
| | Acts 8:26–29 | An angel leads Philip to the Ethiopian eunuch. |
| | Acts 8:30–38 | Eunuch reads Isaiah to Philip; Philip teaches him of Jesus and baptizes him. |
| | Acts 8:39–40 | Spirit leads Philip to teach in Azotus. |
| A.D. 31 | Acts 9:32–35 | Peter visits all parts of the Church; heals Aeneas. |
| | Acts 9:36–43 | Peter brings Tabitha (Dorcas) back to life. |
| A.D. 40 | Acts 10:1–8 | Cornelius sees angel in vision who tells him to get Peter. |
| | Acts 10:9–16 | Peter sees vision of unclean animals. |
| | Acts 10:17–48 | Peter goes to Cornelius, a Gentile, and delivers sermon. |
| | Acts 11:1–18 | Peter announces change in Church doctrine toward Gentiles. |
| | Acts 11:26 | "Christian" title for disciples started at Antioch. |
| | Acts 11:29–30 | Antioch Church sends relief to Jerusalem Church. |
| A.D. 44 | Acts 12:1–2 | Herod kills James with the sword, the first Apostle to be killed.. |
| | Acts 12:3–11 | Peter jailed; an angel leads Peter out of prison and past the guards. |
| | Acts 12:12–17 | Peter tells his escape story to Mary. |

# The Triumphs of the Twelve

| Date | Scripture | Occurrence |
|------|-----------|------------|
| A.D. 44 (cont.) | Acts 12:18–23 | Herod smitten by angel and dies of worms. |
| | Acts 13:5 | John ministered at Salomis, near Isle of Patmos. Word of God grew. |
| A.D. 46 | Acts 15:6–12 | Question of circumcision debated by Apostles and elders. |
| | Acts 15:13–21 | James gives decision on circumcision debate. |
| | Acts 15:22–35 | Letters are sent to all churches with official position on circumcision. |
| A.D. 54 | Acts 21:18 | Paul reports to James in Jerusalem. |

# FAITH AND WORKS

# FAITH AND WORKS

*Cross Referencing System, ScriptureKIT, Book 2* by Bruce Barton

| No. | Description | Scripture |
|-----|-------------|-----------|
| 1 | Naaman's faith and works heal him. | 2 Kings 5:1–4 |
| 2 | Daniel, in the lion's den, showed faith. | Daniel 6 |
| 3 | Centurion's faith and servant's healing. | Matt. 8:5–13 |
| 4 | Faith and ordinances are connected. | Matt. 8:8–13 |
| 5 | Faith likened to a seed (parable). | Matt. 13:31 Alma 32:26–43 |
| 6 | Peter walks on water, then faith fails. | Matt. 14:28–30 |
| 7 | Faith can move mountains. | Matt. 17:20 |
| 8 | A lack of faith affects miracles. | Mark 6:1–16 |
| 9 | Signs follow believers. | Mark 16:17–18 |
| 10 | Faith healed a woman who touched Jesus' robes. | Luke 8:43–48 |
| 11 | Peter's faith and prayer raises a dead woman. | Acts 9:36–42 |
| 12 | We walk by faith, not by sight. | 2 Cor. 5:7 |
| 13 | By faith, worlds were created. | Heb. 11:3 |
| 14 | Faith without works is dead. | James 2:14–26 |
| 15 | The Liahona worked by faith and heed. | 1 Nephi 16:28 |
| 16 | Faith is not a perfect knowledge. | Alma 32:21 |

# Faith and Works

| No. | Description | Scripture |
| --- | --- | --- |
| 17 | Great things come to those with faith. | Ether 4:7–19 |
| 18 | Ye receive no witness until faith is tried. | Ether 12:6 |
| 19 | Principles of miracles explained. | Mormon 9 |
| 20 | Lord works with men according to their faith. | Moroni 10:7 |
| 21 | "Faith cometh, not by signs, but…" | D&C 63:9 |

# WOMEN AND THE WORK

# WOMEN AND THE WORK

| Name | Scripture | About |
|------|-----------|-------|
| Anna | Luke 2:36–38 | An aged widow who continually served God in the temple, testified that the son of Mary was the Christ. |
| Candace of Ethiopia | Acts 8:27 | Her court eunuch was converted by Philip. |
| Chloe | 1 Cor. 1:11 | Warned Paul of contentions among Church members. |
| Damarias | Acts 17:34 | Converted by Paul. |
| Dorcas Tabitha | Acts 9:36–42 | A disciple who shared all she had with the needy. Peter returned her to life after she had died. |
| Drusilla and Bernice | Acts 24:24–25 Acts 25:13,23 | Sisters; daughters of Herod Agrippa who persecuted the Church. |
| Elisabeth | Luke 1:5–80 | Mary's cousin, wife of Zacharias. Angel Gabriel tells her she will have a son after many childless years called John. |
| Eunice and Lois | 2 Tim. 1:5–7 | Mother and grandmother to Timothy. |
| Euodia and Syntyche | Philip. 4:2 | Sisters who labored with Paul. |

| 𝔑ame | 𝔖cripture | 𝔄bout |
|------|-----------|-------|
| Herodias | Matt. 14:3–12 | Granddaughter of Herod the Great. John the Baptist condemned her for an incestuous marriage. She had her daughter, Salome, dance before Herod, who promised her anything; she asked for the head of John the Baptist. |
| Joanna | Luke 8:3<br>Luke 24:10 | Wife of Chuza, Herod's steward. Jesus healed her of an evil spirit. She was also at the tomb. |
| Lydia | Acts 16:14–15, 40 | Converted herself and then her entire household. Supported and helped the Apostles. |
| Mary | Matt. 1:16–23<br>Matt. 2:11<br>Matt. 13:55<br>Matt. 27:56<br>Matt. 28:1<br>Mark 6:3<br>Mark 15:40, 47<br>Mark 16:1–8<br>Luke 1:27–56<br>Luke 2:5,16,19, 33,34<br>Luke 24:10<br>John 19:25<br>Acts 1:14<br>1 Ne.11:13,15, 18–20<br>Mosiah 3:8<br>Alma 7:10<br>Alma 19:13 | Mother of Jesus, James, Joses, Simon Zelotes, and Judas. Mother of unnumbered and unnamed daughters. Married to Joseph. Sister to Salome. Entrusted to John at Christ's death. |
| Mary, the mother of John Mark | Acts 12:12–13 | Peter briefly came to her home after an angel released him. It was a gathering place for Christians. |

## Women and the Work

| 𝕹ame | 𝕾cripture | 𝕬bout |
|------|-----------|-------|
| Mary Magdalene | Matt. 27:56–61<br>Matt. 28:1<br>Mark 15:40,47<br>Mark 16:1, 9, 10<br>Luke 8:2<br>Luke 24:10<br>John 19:25<br>John 20:1,11, 16,18 | Healed by Jesus of "seven devils." She was at the cross when he was crucified. She was the first to see the risen Christ. |
| Mary and Martha | Mark 14:3–9<br>Luke 10:38–42<br>John 11<br>John 12:1–9 | Sisters who lived in Bethany. Their brother was Lazarus, whom Jesus raised from the dead. Known for the story where Martha prepared the meal while Mary listened to Jesus. Both were loyal supporters of Jesus and his ministry. |
| Mary, wife of Cleophas | Matt. 27:56–61<br>John 19:25 | She was at the cross with Mary (Jesus' mother), Salome (Mary's sister) and Mary Magadalene. |
| Peter's wife, and her mother | Matt. 8:14–15 | Jesus sometimes stayed in her home. He healed her mother of a fever. She was martyred with Peter and Paul. |
| Phebe (Phoebe) | Romans 16:1–2 | A servant of the Church. Carried a letter for Paul. |
| Philip's four virgin daughters | Acts 21:8–9 | Prophetesses. Paul visited their home in Caesarea. |
| Priscilla | Acts 18:2–28 | Taught the gospel with her husband Aquila. Converted Apollos. |

# The Triumphs of the Twelve

| Name | Scripture | About |
|---|---|---|
| Procula, wife of Pilate | Matt. 27:19 (not named) | Because of a dream, she spoke out for Jesus on the day of his trial. |
| Rhoda | Acts 12:13 | She left Peter knocking at the house gate. |
| Roman women | Romans 16:6–15 2 Tim. 4:21 Phil. 1:2 | Personal greeting to individuals. |
| Salome | Matt. 27:56 (not named) Mark 15:40 Mark 16:1 John 19:25 ("his mother's sister") | Wife of Zebedee, mother to James and John. Christ's aunt (Mary's sister). |
| Salome, daughter of Herodias | Matt. 14:6–11 Mark 6:22–28 | Demanded and got head of John the Baptist as reward for dancing. |
| Sapphira | Acts 5:1–11 | Married to Ananias. They said they gave all to the Church, but lied and were struck dead. |
| Sisters of Jesus | Matt. 13:55–56 | Unnamed and unnumbered daughters of Joseph and Mary. |
| Susanna | Luke 8:2–3 | Healed by Jesus of evil spirits. She was one of the first to see the resurrected Christ. |
| Syrophenician woman | Matt. 15:21–28 | Her plea for His crumbs persuaded Jesus to heal her daughter. |
| Weeping women at the Crucifixion | Luke 23:28 | Women were often paid to lament at funerals. |

# Women and the Work

| Name | Scripture | About |
|------|-----------|-------|
| Woman healed on the Sabbath | Luke 13:11–16 | Woman was bowed with infirmity for 18 years. |
| Woman with 12-year issue of blood | Matt. 9:20–22 | Faith prompted her to touch the hem of Jesus' garment. |
| Woman taken in adultery | John 8:3–11 | Caught by others but forgiven by Jesus. |
| Woman at the well | John 4:7–43 | Samaritan sinner tells her village of Christ. |

# Roles of Women

꧁꧂

| Scripture | Role |
|---|---|
| Gen. 1:27–28 | God created men & women to be… |
| Gen. 2:18, 21–24<br>Moses 3:20–24<br>Abr. 5:14–18 | God created woman to be helpmeet. |
| Gen. 3:20, 16<br>Moses 4:26,22 | Eve is the first "mother" of all living. |
| Exodus 15:20 (Miriam)<br>Judges 4,5 (Deborah)<br>2 Kings 22:14 (Huldah)<br>2 Chron. 34:22 (Huldah)<br>Neh. 6:14 (Noadiah)<br>Luke 2:36 (Anna)<br>Acts 21:9 (4 daughters of Philip) | Prophetesses. |
| Num. 30:3–5 | If a daughter vow… |
| Num. 30:6–8, 10–15 | If a wife vow… |
| Num. 30:9 | If a widow or divorcee vow… |
| Judges 4,5 | Deborah was prophetess, judge, and chieftess. |
| Esther 4:13–14 | "…thou art…for such a time as this…" |
| Prov. 31:10–31 | …a virtuous woman… |
| Matt. 27:55–56<br>Luke 8:1–3; 23:55 | Women traveled with Jesus and Apostles to care for them. |
| Proverbs 31:10–31<br>Acts 16:14–15,40 | Women manage households and businesses. |

# Roles of Women

| Scripture | Role |
| --- | --- |
| Matt. 27:55–56,61<br>Luke 23:55–56<br>John 20:1–2 | Women ministered to Christ and anointed His body after His death. |
| Mark 15:47<br>Luke 23:55–56 | Women saw to His burial. |
| Matt. 28:1–8<br>Mark 16:1–8<br>Luke 24:1–12 | Women were the first to see the resurrected Christ. |
| Luke 24:22–24 | Women saw vision of angels. |
| Acts 13:50; 17:4 | Chief women help rule cities. |
| Acts 17:12 | Women believed Christ. |
| Acts 18:26–28 | Women clarified doctrine of Christ. |
| Mark 15:40, 41<br>1 Cor. 9:5 | Women were important helpmeets to Apostles. |
| 1 Peter 3:1–7 | Christian marriage. |
| Jacob 2:27–28 | God delights in chastity. |
| Mosiah 10:4–5 | Work of men and women. |
| D&C 25 | An elect lady. |
| D&C 83:1–3, 6 | Claims of women on the Church. |

# New Testament
# Prayers and
# Proclamations

# New Testament Prayers and Proclamations

| Prayers/Events/ Proclamations | Offered by | Scripture |
|---|---|---|
| Baptism of Jesus | Voice from heaven | Matt 3:13 Luke 3:22 |
| Sermon on the Mount | Jesus Christ | Matt 5–7 |
| The Lord's Prayer | Jesus Christ | Matt. 6:9–13 |
| Thanks to Father | Jesus Christ | Matt. 11:25–27 |
| "Thou art the Christ" | Peter | Matt. 16:16 Mark 8:29 Luke 9:20 |
| Mount of Transfiguration | Voice from heaven | Matt. 17:5 Luke 9:35,36 |
| In Gethsemene | Jesus Christ | Matt. 26:39–42 |
| Of Jesus as Son of God | Roman Centurion, Manlius[17] | Matt. 27:54 Mark 15:39 Luke 23:47 |
| "He is risen" | Angel | Matt. 28:1–7 Mark 16:1–8 Luke 24:1–7 |
| How to pray | Jesus Christ | Mark 11:22–26 |
| False Christs | Jesus Christ | Mark 13:5–37 |

# The Triumphs of the Twelve

| Prayers/Events/Proclamations | Offered by | Scripture |
|---|---|---|
| To Zacharias | Angel Gabriel | Luke 1:13–17 |
| To Mary | Angel Gabriel | Luke 1:30–33 |
| Upon greeting Mary | Elisabeth | Luke 1:42–45 |
| Upon the Annunciation | Mary, mother of Jesus | Luke 1:46–55 |
| Upon birth of John the Baptist | Zacharias | Luke 1:67–79 |
| To shepherds | Angel Gabriel and heavenly host | Luke 2:10–14 |
| Naming baby Jesus | Simeon | Luke 2:25–35 |
| Naming baby Jesus | Anna, a prophetess | Luke 2:36–38 |
| In Nazareth | Jesus Christ | Luke 4:16–22 |
| To Jesus | Unclean devils | Luke 4:33, 34, 41 |
| Before calling the Twelve Apostles | Jesus Christ | Luke 6:12 |
| To Jesus | Legion of devils | Luke 8:27–39 |
| Signs of the Last Days | Jesus Christ | Luke 21:5–36 |
| Remove cup | Jesus Christ | Luke 22:42 |
| For Jerusalem | Jesus Christ | Luke 23:27–31 |
| For His murderers | Jesus Christ | Luke 23:34 |
| For two thieves | Jesus Christ | Luke 23:43 |
| To His Father | Jesus Christ | Luke 23:46 |
| First visit after Resurrection | Jesus Christ | Luke 24:36–51 |
| Of Jesus | John the Baptist | John 1:29–34 |
| "Thou art the Son of God" | Nathanael | John 1:49 |
| To Jesus | Nicodemus | John 3:1–2 |
| To Nicodemus | Jesus Christ | John 3:3, 5–21 |

# New Testament Prayers and Proclamations

| Prayers/Events/Proclamations | Offered by | Scripture |
|---|---|---|
| Born again | Jesus Christ | John 3:1–21 |
| Believe on Christ | John the Baptist | John 3:25–36 |
| To the Samaritan woman at the well | Jesus Christ | John 4:10–14, 21–26 |
| Father's will | Jesus Christ | John 5:19–47 |
| Bread of Life | Jesus Christ | John 6:32–65 |
| Temple teachings | Jesus Christ | John 7 and 8 |
| To the healed man born blind | Jesus Christ | John 9:37 |
| "I am the door of the sheepfold" | Jesus Christ | John 10:1–5 John 10:7–18 John 10:25–30 |
| "Ye are Gods" | Jesus Christ | John 10:34–38 |
| "Thou art the Christ" | Martha | John 11:27 |
| Thanks His Father for listening | Jesus Christ | John 11:41–42 |
| His Father's name glorified | Jesus Christ | John 12:23–28 |
| To Jesus, Apostles, and Greeks | Voice from heaven | John 12:28–32 |
| Intercessory Prayer | Jesus Christ | John 17 |
| Final proclamation | Jesus Christ | Acts 1:6–9 |
| Second Coming | Two angels | Acts 1:10–11 |
| On choosing Judas' successor | Eleven Apostles | Acts 1:24–26 |
| For help in persecution | Church members | Acts 4:23–33 |
| For pardon of his murderers | Stephen | Acts 7:54–60 |
| Peter's vision then conversion of Gentiles | Voice from heaven | Acts 10:9–48; 11:1–18 |

# The Triumphs of the Twelve

| Prayers/Events/ Proclamations | Offered by | Scripture |
| --- | --- | --- |
| Jesus died and is resurrected | Paul | Acts 13:27–37 |
| (Paul and Silas) are servants of the Most High God | Damsel of divination | Acts 16:16–18 |
| Preaches of the unknown God | Paul | Acts 17:22–34 |
| "Jesus…and Paul I know…" | Evil spirit | Acts 19:3–16 |

# ENDNOTES

1. McBirnie, *The Search for the Twelve Apostles.*
2. Talmage, *Jesus the Christ*, 109. "In treating this topic Dr. Charles F. Deems (*The Light of the Nations*, p. 28), after giving careful consideration of the estimates, calculations, and assumptions of men who have employed many means in their investigation and reach only discordant results says: 'It is annoying to see learned men use the same apparatus of calculation and reach the most diverse results. It is bewildering to attempt a reconciliation of these varying calculations.' In an appended note the same author states, 'For example: the birth of our Lord is placed in B.C. 1 by Pearson and Hug; B.C. 2 by Scalinger; B.C. 3 by Baronius and Paulus; B.C. 4 by Bengel, Wieseler, and Greswell; B.C. 5 by Usher and Petavius; B.C. 6 by Strong, Luvin, and Clark; B.C. 7 by Ideler and Sanclemente.'"
3. McBirnie, *The Search for the Twelve Apostles.*
4. Durant, *Caesar and Christ*, 578 and 692. "His parents gave him the quite common name Yeshu'a (our Joshua), meaning 'the help of Yahveh'; the Greeks made this into *Iesous*, the Romans into *Iesus*."
5. Barton, *ScriptureKIT Book 1:Information Pages*,™ "Sources" by Byron Lee Borup, 17.
6. Talmage, *Jesus the Christ*, 224. "Concerning the Jameses mentioned in the New Testament, the opinion of Bible scholars is divided, the question being as to whether two or three individuals are indicated. Those who hold that there were three men of

this name distinguish them as follows: (1) James the son of Zebedee and brother of John the apostle; all scriptural references to him are explicit; (2) James the son of Alpheus; and (3) James the brother of the Lord (Matt. 13:55; Mark 6:3; Gal. 1:19 . . . Both the Oxford and Bagster Bible "Helps" treat James the son of Alpheus and James the Lord's brother as one person, the expression 'son of' being understood in its general sense only. . . . The Bagster designation is: 'James II, apostle, son of Alpheus, brother or cousin to Jesus'. . . . The Nave 'Student's Bible' states . . . that the question as to whether James the Lord's brother 'is identical with James the son of Alpheus is one of the most difficult questions in the biographical history of the Gospels.' Faussett . . . supports the contention that but one James is meant; and other acknowledged authorities treat the two as one." Also on page 229, footnote 3: "In all Bible passages specifying 'James son of Alpheus' (Matt. 10:3; Mark 3:18; Luke 6:15; Acts 1:13) the word *son* . . . appears in *italics*. The phrase in the Greek reads 'James of Alpheus.' This fact must not be given undue weight in support of the thought that the James spoken of was not the son of Alpheus; for the word *son* has been similarly added in the translation of other passages, in all of which *italics* are used to indicate the words supplied, e.g. 'James *the son* of Zebedee.'"

7. Talmage, *Jesus the Christ*, 69. "This [the Sanhedrin], the chief court or high council of the Jews, derives its name from Greek *sunedrion*, signifying 'a council.' In English it is sometimes though inaccurately written 'Sanhedrim.' The Talmud traces the origins of this body to the calling of the seventy elders whom Moses associated with himself, making seventy-one in all, to administer as judges in Israel (Numb. 11:16,17). The Sanhedrin in the time of Christ, as also long before, comprized [sic] seventy-one members, including the high priest who presided in the assembly."

8. *The Archko Volume*, 80.

9. Eisenmann, *James, the Brother of Jesus*, 466–520, 553–597.

10. Durant, *Caesar and Christ*, 582. Shows that the name *Christian* did not come into use until the second half of the first century. Prior to this, followers of Christ were referred to as "Believers," "Disciples," "Brethren" or "Saints." The term Christian comes from the scornful name *Christianoi*—meaning "Followers of the Messiah or the Anointed One." As an interesting aside, the term *gentile* comes from the Latin term *gente*, meaning people or nations.

11. Keller, *The Bible as History.*

12. Jowett, *The Drama of the Lost Disciples*, 176. Quoted in McBirnie, *The Search for the Twelve Apostles*, 65–66.

13. McBirnie, *The Search For The Twelve Apostles.* "In 1939, while excavations were being made for Pius XI's tomb, Pius XII gave orders that the digging was to be extended in a search for the tomb of St. Peter.

"A Roman presbyter named Gaius, who lived in the second and third centuries, had seen a grave memorial to St. Peter, and had mentioned it in a letter, a fragment of which has come down to us. Right under the papal altar, early in the excavations, a small ruined monument was found. They found a grave, but it was quite empty.

"Margherita Guarducci is a professor at the University of Rome, and she deciphers ancient inscriptions.

"She spent six years studying the scribblings made by Christian pilgrims on two old walls above the empty grave. One graffito on the older wall, when deciphered, delivered an electrifying message: 'Peter is within.' In the other wall was a recess lined with marble. To her it was clearly an ossuary, a niche for someone's bones. Had any been found?

"She searched St. Peter's storage rooms. There in a box marked for graffiti, she found bones.

"It was plain to her what had happened. When Constantine built the first St. Peter's, he had cautiously moved the bones of the Saint from his grave to this hiding place, a few feet away, to protect them from deterioration and grave robbers. Much later, a monsignor, during an inspection, had put the bones in a plain wood box and deposited it in storage.

"That the bones Professor Guarducci found are those of St. Peter, she has no doubt. They are the bones of a man of 60 or 70, and in a box with them were bits of earth and shreds of purple-and-gold cloth. The age tallies with Peter's traditional age at the time of his crucifixion. And when Constantine had the bones removed to the niche, it would have seemed only fitting to have had them wrapped in precious purple-and-gold cloth.

"Scholars disputed these conclusions; some still do. But Pope Paul VI settled the question for the Catholic world. Speaking in St. Peter's on June 26, 1968, he announced that the bones of the saint had been found.

"Today the bones are back in the niche of the tomb, hidden from public view." (*National Geographic*, "St. Peter's" by Aubrey Menen, Vol. 140, No. 6, December, 1971, 872,873)."

14. *The Archko Volume,* 86–87. "Gamaliel's Interview with Joseph & Mary & Others Concerning Jesus."

"It seems that Joseph and Mary think that the Sanhedrin should do something for Him (Jesus) to get Him out and let Him show Himself to the people. I (Gamaliel) tried to console them by telling them that my understanding of the prophecy was that He had come to the high priesthood first, and there to work in the spiritual dominion of the heart; and when He had brought about a unity of heart and oneness of aim, it would be easy enough to establish His political claim; and all who would not willingly submit to Him, it would be an easy matter with the sword of Joshua or Gideon to bring under His control.

"It seemed to me that His parents' ideas are of a selfish character; that they care nothing about the Jewish government nor the Roman oppression. But I told them they were mistaken; that the building up of the Kingdom of Heaven was not to be done by might nor by power, but by the Spirit of the Lord, and it would not do for us to use carnal weapons, nor to expect carnal pleasures to be derived therefrom; that it was not my understanding of the prophecy that this King was to use such weapons either for Himself or for the benefit of a party, but for the good of all men; that His dominion was to be universal, and it was to be of a spiritual character; that He was sent to the lost and not to the found."

15. *The Archko Volume*, 87–88. "His [Jesus'] parents told me of an old man who lived on the road to Bethany who had once been a priest, a man of great learning, and well skilled in the laws and the prophets, and that Jesus was often there with him reading the law and the prophets together; that his name was Massalian, and that I might find Jesus there. But he was not there. I asked him [Massalian] to give me an outline of the character of Jesus. He said that he was a young man of the finest thought and feeling he ever saw in his life; that he was the most apt in his answers and solutions of difficult problems of any man of his age he had ever seen; that his answers seem to give more universal satisfaction— so much so that the oldest philosopher would not dispute with him, or in any manner join issue with him, or ask the second time. I asked Massalian who taught him to read and interpret the law and the prophets. He said that his mother said that he had always known how to read the law; that his mind seemed to master it from the beginning; and into the laws of nature and the relation of man to his fellow in his teachings or talks, he gives a deeper insight, inspiring mutual love and strengthening the common trust of society. Another plan he has of setting men right with the laws of nature: he turns nature into a great law book of illustrations, showing that every bush is a flame, every rock a foundation of water, every star a pillar of fire, and every cloud the one that leads to God. He makes all nature preach the doctrine of trust in the divine Fatherhood . . ."

16. In Deuteronomy 21:22–23, Jews are told that if a man is crucified—dies hanged on a tree—then he really was guilty of that crime. Thus, Thomas had scriptural reason to doubt that his Lord had actually come back to life.

Jesus, being condemned by the Jews as a perversion of the Jewish laws had to die at human hands to fulfill the demands of mercy for all men. He went up to the heavenly courts, received His justification of that heavenly council, then returned to His followers to instruct them for 40 days with more "good news."

After those 40 days, the Twelve and other followers are truly converted and live out the rest of their lives testifying of our Savior.

17. *The Archko Volume.* 131–132, 147. "Acta Pilati, or Pilate's Report to Caesar [Tiberius] of the Arrest, Trial, and Crucifixion of Jesus."

"My secretary's name is Manlius. He is the grandson of the chief of the conspirators who encamped in Etruria waiting for Cataline. Manlius had been for a long time an inhabitant of Judea, and is well acquainted with the Hebrew language. He was devoted to me, and worthy of my confidence.

"I [Pilate] am almost ready to say, as did Manlius at the cross, 'Truly this was the Son of God.'"

# CHRONOLOGY

| Year | Jewish /Idumaean History | Roman History |
|---|---|---|
| 48 B.C. / A.M.* 3714 | • Antipater is made procurator of Judea.† <br> • His son, Herod, is made governor of Galilee, with the task of clearing Galilean Zealots. | • Caesar defeats Pompey at the Battle of Pharsalus. <br> • Ptolemy XII of Egypt murders Pompey. <br> • Caesar lays siege to Alexandria on behalf of Queen Cleopatra. |
| 47 B.C. / A.M. 3715 | • Son Herod is made a Roman citizen, along with his brothers. | • Caesar defeats Cleopatra's rivals for the Egyptian throne, Ptolemy XIII and Arsinoe IV. <br> • Caesar invades Africa. |
| 46 B.C. / A.M. 3716 | • *Jews who supported Caesar are granted many privileges, such as exemption from emperor worship, from military service, and from certain taxes.‡* <br> • *"In the times of the Maccabees, they bravely fought on Sabbaths and routed their foreign enemies..." (Tertullian, c. 197).* | • Caesar enters Rome triumphantly with his mistress, Cleopatra. He is made dictator for ten years. <br> • Caesar becomes Pontifex Maximus, and in this role **reforms the Roman calendar** to a 365 day calendar with an extra day every 4 years. <br> • Caesar appoints his nephew Octavian his heir. |
| 45 B.C. / A.M. 3717 | • Caesar relies on Antipater and Hyrcanus, of Hasmonean lineage, for support. | • Caesar defeats Pompey's forces in Spain. <br> • Caesar now dictator for life. |

*A.M.–Anno Mundi (Hebrew dating system starting from creation of the world)
†Events–regular type    ‡ Cultural tidbits–italic type

# The Triumphs of the Twelve

| Year | Jewish /Idumaean History | Roman History |
|---|---|---|
| 44 B.C. / A.M. 3718 | • Hyrcanus, high priest, is made "Prince of the Jews." <br> • Antipater rebuilds the walls of Jerusalem. | • Caesar assassinated. <br> • Octavian returns from Apollonia to take up Caesar's inheritance. <br> • Mark Antony stakes his claim against Octavian. |
| 43 B.C. / 3719 | • Antipater is poisoned. <br> • Cassius plunders Jerusalem. | • Mark Antony, Marcus Lepidus, and Octavian form the 2nd Triumvirate. Antony orders Cicero's assassination. |
| 42 B.C. / A.M. 3720 | • Antigonus creates disturbances in Judea, but is quelled by Herod. <br> • Herod enters Jerusalem in triumph. He is betrothed to Mariamne of the Hasmonean dynasty. | • Caesar recognized as a god. <br> • Octavian and Antony defeat Cassius and Marcus Brutus at Philippi, who commit suicide. |
| 41 B.C. / A.M. 3721 | • Antony makes Herod and his brother Phasael, tetrarchs. | • Antony meets Cleopatra in Cilicia. <br> • Lucius Antonius and Fulvia, brother and wife of Mark Antony, incite the War of the Veterans. |
| 40 B.C. / A.M. 3722 | • Parthians slay Phasael, brother of Herod, imprison Hyrcanus, and appoint Antigonus king of Judea. <br> • Herod flees to Rome and is there constituted king by the senate and by Antony. | • Lucius Antonius and Fulvia are defeated. <br> • Antony and Octavian divide the Roman world between them. Antony controls the East and Octavian the West. Lepidus takes control of Africa. |

# Chronology

| Year | Jewish /Idumaean History | Roman History |
|---|---|---|
| 39 B.C. / A.M. 3723 | • Herod returns to fight Jerusalem at the beginning of his war against Antigonus, with a Roman army at his command. Parthians support Antigonus against the Romans under Herod. | • Publius Ventidius defeats the Parthians in Cilicia.<br>• Sextus Pompieus controls Sicily, Sardinia, Corsica, and the Peloponnese. The Triumvirs formally recognize these possessions in return for Pompieus's halt to interruptions of Rome's grain supply.<br>• The first public library is founded. |
| 38 B.C. / A.M. 3724 | • Herod continues his war against Jerusalem. | • Treaty of Tarentum extends 2nd Triumvirate until 33 B.C. |
| 37 B.C. / A.M. 3725 | • Herod the Great (37–4 B.C.) takes Jerusalem. He banishes his first wife, Doris, and their three-year-old son, and marries Mariamne.<br>• Antigonus is executed by Antony.<br>• Annel is made high priest. | • Octavian provides Antony with troops for the war against the Parthians.<br>• The Romans drive the Parthians (Persians) from Jerusalem. |
| 36 B.C. / A.M. 3726 | • Herod makes Anamelus high priest at the request of Cleopatra of Egypt. | • Antony goes to live with Cleopatra in Egypt, and marries her despite already being married to Octavia, Octavian's sister. |
| 35 B.C. / A.M. 3727 | • Herod deposes Anamelus and appoints Aristobulus, his wife's brother, to the high priesthood.<br>• Aristobulus drowns at a party. It is not known if Herod had him killed. | • Death of Sallust.<br>• Illyria, in the Balkans, becomes a Roman province.<br>• Pannonia (modern Hungary) is attacked by Octavian. |

| Year | Jewish /Idumaean History | Roman History |
|------|--------------------------|---------------|
| 34 B.C. / A.M. 3728 | • Herod appeases Antony and Cleopatra with large presents, including Coele-Syria, and rare plants for Cleopatra's palace, with Hebrew gardeners to tend them for years. | • Antony gives Coele-Syria (southern Syria) to Cleopatra.<br>• Antony establishes Cleopatra as a Hellenistic monarch at Alexandria. |
| 33 B.C. / A.M. 3729 | • Herod is nicknamed "the Great" for his many building improvements. | • *Rich Roman girls marry between 12 and 14.* |
| 32 B.C. / A.M. 3730 | • Herod goes to war against Nabatea, making good use of his strongholds named after various family members, e.g., Cypros, and Herodium. | • Octavian arouses fears that Antony is controlled by Cleopatra. He arranges for Italy, Gaul, Spain, and Africa to make oaths of alliance to him. He has Antony's authority annulled.<br>• Antony divorces Octavia. |
| 31 B.C. / A.M. 3731 | • At Antony's insistence, Herod subdues Malchus, king of Arabia Petrea.<br>• Earthquake in Judea.<br>• Herod switches alliances to Octavian after Antony's defeat.<br>• Masada is completed by Herod. | • Octavian declares war on Antony and Cleopatra. They are defeated at Actium.<br>• Antony, believing that Cleopatra has died, commits suicide.<br>• *Many marriages are arranged, but can be dissolved by mutual consent of the couple.* |
| 30 B.C. / A.M. 3732 | • Herod makes peace with Octavian. He is confirmed in his kingdom.<br>• *"The prophets are full of acknowledged difficulties and of declarations that are obscure to the multitude..." (Origen, c. 248 E).* | • Octavian captures Alexandria.<br>• Cleopatra attempts to seduce. Octavian. She commits suicide after her failure to do so.<br>• Ptolemy XV Caesarion is murdered. He is believed to be the only son of Julius Caesar. |

# Chronology

| Year | Jewish /Idumaean History | Roman History |
|---|---|---|
| 29 B.C. / A.M. 3733 | • Herod becomes jealous of Mariamne and has her put to death. | • A temple in the Forum is dedicated to Julius Caesar. |
| 28 B.C. / A.M. 3734 | • Herod executes his brother-in-law, Kostobar, for conspiracy. • He also executes his mother-in-law, Alexandra. | • 82 Roman temples are restored. • *Poorer Roman girls, whose husbands could not afford slaves, marry in late teens or early 20s.* |
| 27 B.C. / A.M. 3735 | • An assassination attempt on Herod is uncovered. • Herod rebuilds Samaria and renames it Sebaste, in honor of Augustus. | • The name Augustus is conferred upon Octavian. As Caesar Augustus, he rules until his suspicious death in A.D. 14. • Pantheon is built in Rome and still stands intact. In A.D. 608, it becomes a Christian church. |
| 26 B.C. / A.M. 3736 | • Herod murders the last of the family of Hyrcanus. | • Rome obtains control of the Hispania peninsula. |
| 25 B.C. / A.M. 3737 | • There is drought in Judea. Herod imports grain from Egypt, begins an aid program, and waives a third of the taxes. | • Petronius secures frontiers between Egypt and Ethiopia. • Galatia (central Turkey) becomes a Roman province. • Livy begins history of Rome. |
| 24 B.C. / A.M. 3738 | • Herod completes a palace for himself on Mount Zion and erects fortress strongholds. | • Augustus founds the city of Nicopolis in Egypt. • Augustus acquires dominion over the whole Roman Empire. |
| 23 B.C. / A.M. 3739 | • Herod marries his third wife, the second Mariamne. | • Romans invade Kush (Sudan) and sack its capital, Napata. |
| 22 B.C. / A.M. 3740 | • Herod begins to build Caesarea. | • Horace finished his first three books of odes. |

| 𝔜ear | 𝔍ewish /𝔍dumaean 𝔥istory | 𝔯oman 𝔥istory |
|---|---|---|
| 21 B.C. / A.M. 3741 | • *"Herod, knowing that the lineage of the Israelites contributed nothing to him, and goaded by the consciousness of his ignoble birth, burned the [Hebrew] registers of their families. This he did, thinking that he would appear to be of noble birth"* (Julius Africanus, c. 245, E, 6.127). | • *"In our case, you actually conduct trials contrary to the usual form of judicial process against criminals. For when culprits are brought up for trial, if they deny the charge, you press them for a confession by tortures. However, when Christians confess without compulsion, you apply torture to them…"* (Tertullian, c. 197 W). |
| 20 B.C. / A.M. 3742 | • Philo, Jewish writer, is born (d. A.D. 50). | • Peace treaty between Rome and Parthia.<br>• Horace finishes first books of epistles. |
| 19 B.C. / A.M. 3743 | • Herod prepares to renovate the temple in Jerusalem. | • The Spanish campaign ends in a decisive victory for Augustus. |
| 18 B.C. / A.M. 3744 | • Herod travels to Rome for the second time. | • Augustus propagates the *Lex Julia adulterias coercindis*, making public infidelity a crime. |
| 17 B.C. / A.M. 3745 | • Herod begins the work of rebuilding the temple of Jerusalem. It is not finalized until A.D. 63. | • Augustus orders the "ludi saeculares" celebrated in Rome, marking the end of one era and the beginning of another. |
| 16 B.C. / A.M. 3746 | • *"They [the Jews] suppose that the everlasting kingdom will be assuredly given to those of the Dispersion who are of Abraham after the flesh—even though they are sinners, are faithless, and are disobedient towards God. However, the Scriptures have proved this is not the case"* (Justin Martyr, c. 160, E 1.269). | • *"I will write and show how and for what cause images were made to kings and tyrants, and how they came to be regarded as gods…the people of Acte worshipped Dionysius, a king, because he had recently planted the vine. The Egyptians worshiped Joseph the [Jewish] hero, who was called Serapis, because he supplied them with corn during the years of famine"* (Melito, c. 170, E). |

# Chronology

# The Triumphs of the Twelve

| 𝔜ear | 𝔍ewish /𝔍dumaean 𝔥istory | 𝔕oman 𝔥istory |
|------|---------------------------|---------------|
| 9 B.C. / A.M. 3753 | • Herod falls into disgrace with Augustus. He again suspects Alexander intends to kill him. | • Death of Drusus, stepson of Augustus<br>• Tiberius succeeds Drusus as commander of the German campaign.<br>• An altar of peace is dedicated in Rome. |
| 8 B.C. / A.M. 3754 | • Herod accuses his sons by the first Mariamne of high treason.<br>• He is reconciled with Augustus, and proceeds legally against his sons. | • Deaths of Horace and Maecenas, strong friends in the literary advancement of the Roman Empire. Horace wrote "satires," "odes," and more. |
| 7 B.C. / A.M. 3755 | • A hearing is held in Beirut against Herod's sons. They are found guilty and executed.<br>• Conjunction of the planets Saturn and Jupiter within the constellation Pisces, giving the appearance of a great new star. | • *Roman law bars celibates above a certain age and widowers below a certain age who do not remarry from attending public games and from receiving nonfamily inheritances.* |
| 6 B.C. / A.M. 3756 | • The Pharisees refuse the oath to Caesar and are fined.<br>• Double eclipse of Jupiter in Aries on March 20, again on April 16.<br>• The Angel Gabriel appears to Zacharias and promises him a son, John, and strikes him dumb for unbelief.<br>• Herod proceeds harshly against the Pharisees, who announced that the birth of the Messiah would mean the end of his rule. | • Tiberius in Rhodes, then sent to Armenia.<br>• *Property of rich Roman wives is separate from that of their husbands.*<br>• *Only the woman's dowry goes to her husband, and while a bride's father is duty-bound to provide a dowry, it is not mandatory.*<br>• *If a man invaded another's wedlock, the Julian law would visit its adulterous violator with the death penalty (Tertullian, c. 200 W).* |

# Chronology

| Year | Jewish /Idumaean History | Roman History |
|------|--------------------------|----------------|
| 5 B.C. / A.M. 3757 | • Antipater charged with the intended murder of Herod.<br>• Herod is very ill.<br>• A nova blazes in the skies for 70 days.<br>• Annunciation of Mary.<br>• Birth of John the Baptist. | • *The dowry of a rich Roman daughter is usually 5–10% of her father's estate.*<br>• *If a man violated his sisters, the Papinian law would punish the outrage with all penalties, limb by limb (Tertullian, c. 200 W).* |
| 4 B.C. / A.M. 3758 | • Young Torah students smash a golden eagle, installed by Pontius Pilate, over the entrance to the temple.<br>• Herod executes his son Antipater.<br>• The census or register of families and estates in Judea.<br>• Birth of Jesus Christ.<br>• Visit of the Shepherds.<br>• Visit of the Wise Men.<br>• Flight into Egypt, where the Holy Family reportedly live among Hebrew gardeners to Queen Cleopatra's gardens.<br>• Slaughter of Innocents.<br>• Murder of Zacharias.<br>• Death of Herod.<br>• Archelaus becomes ethnarch of Judea.<br>• Herod Antipas becomes King of Galilee. | • *Emperor Augustus expressed desire to remake Roman morality to be more conservative.*<br>• *However, the main poet, Ovid, age 41, has little interest in his three wives and prefers to pursue other women. He publishes "Ars Amatoria" as a text to have no sexual values other than that of conquest.*<br>• *"The soul is not in itself immortal, O Greeks, but mortal. Yet it is not possible for it to die. If, indeed, it does not know the truth, it dies. It is dissolved with the body, but rises again at last at the end of the world with the body, receiving death by punishment in immortality. But, again, if it acquires the knowledge of God, it does not die" (Tatian, c. 160, E).* |
| 3 B.C. / A.M. 3759 | • Conjunction of Jupiter and Venus. | • *World population reaches roughly 250 million.* |
| 2 B.C. / A.M. 3760 | • Joseph and Mary, with Jesus, return from Egypt and settle at Nazareth. | • Augustus is given the title *pater patriae* (Father of his Country). |

| 𝔜ear | 𝔍ewish /𝔍dumaean 𝔥istory | 𝔯oman 𝔥istory |
|------|--------------------------|---------------|
| A.D. 1 / A.M. 3761 | • Beginning of the "Christian Era." <br> • Archelaus and Antipas are made tetrarchs of Judea. | • Tiberius quells revolts in Germany. <br> • Silk appears in Rome. <br> • Lions become extinct in western Europe. |
| A.D. 2 / A.M. 3762 | • *(The Gnostics) are in all points inconsistent with themselves when they declare that all souls do not enter into the intermediate place, but only those of the "righteous" (Irenaeus, c. 180, E/W).* | • Suspicious death of Lucius Caesar. <br> • Suspicious death of Gaius Caesar. |
| A.D. 3 / A.M. 3763 | • *"We read that every scripture suitable for edification is divinely inspired. So it may now seem to have been rejected by the Jews for that very reason—just like nearly all other portions [of canon] that speak of Christ. Nor, of course, is this fact surprising: that they did not receive some scriptures that spoke of Him whom they did not receive. For they did not receive Him even when He was here in person speaking in their presence" (Tertullian, c. 198, W).* | • *"I think that the corrupting influence of the stage is more contaminating than the circus [gladiator combats]. That is because the subject of comedies is the dishonoring of virgins or the loves of harlots. They persuade others by the elegance of their words. . . In like manner, the tragedies place before the eyes the incests and parental murders of wicked kings. They also portray dire crimes . . . to teach and incite lust . . . They teach adulteries while they act them out" (Lactantius, c. A.D. 304–313).* |
| A.D. 4 / A.M. 3764 | • Judas of Gamala rebels against Rome. He and his followers are caught and crucified. | • Caius, son of Augustus, dies suspiciously at Lycia. <br> • Augustus names stepson Tiberius his heir. |
| A.D. 5 / A.M. 3765 | • Herod's son, Archelaus, rules Judea oppressively. | • Tiberius conquers Germania Inferior. |
| A.D. 6 / A.M. 3766 | • Judea is annexed to the Roman province of Syria. | • Food shortage in Rome. Augustus doubles corn rations. |

# Chronology

| Year | Jewish /Idumaean History | Roman History |
|------|--------------------------|---------------|
| A.D. 7 / A.M. 3767 | • Augustus dismisses Herod Archelaus. | • Revolt of Illyrians, Pannonians, and Dalmatians. |
| A.D. 8 / A.M. 3768 | • Jesus teaches in the temple at the age of 12. | • Ovid is exiled by Augustus for Ovid's immoral practices. |
| A.D. 9 / A.M. 3769 | • Birth of Saul (Paul) of Tarsus. | • Illyria is defeated and becomes a Roman province. Pannonian revolt is crushed. |
| A.D. 10 / A.M. 3770 | • Marcus Ambivius, procurator of Judea. <br> • Birth of Peter (traditional). | • Pannonia (modern Hungary) becomes a Roman province. |
| A.D. 11 / A.M. 3771 | • *"There are various abodes according to the worth of those who have believed"* (Clement of Alexandria, c. 195, E). | • Germania Inferior and the Rhine are secured. |
| A.D. 12 / A.M. 3772 | • Annius Rufus becomes procurator of Judea. | • *"The entire apparatus of the shows is based on adultery"* (Tertullian, c. 197, W). |
| A.D. 13 / A.M. 3773 | • *"The demons who rule over men are not the souls of men"* (Tatian, c. 160, E). | • Tiberius receives a proconsular imperium. |
| A.D. 14 / A.M. 3774 | • *"Indeed, render unto Caesar money. Render to God, yourself. Otherwise, what will be God's if all things are Caesar's?"* (Tertullian, c. 200, W). | • Death of Caesar Augustus on September 14, at age 76. <br> • Tiberius becomes emperor at age 55. <br> • Augustus' adopted son, Agrippa Posthumus, put to death. <br> • Augustus is deified. |
| A.D. 15 / A.M. 3775 | • Valerius Gratus becomes procurator of Judea. | • *"Circuses" refer to chariot races.* |
| A.D. 16 / A.M. 3776 | • *"Those whose speech is evil are not better than those whose actions are evil . . ."* (Clement of Alexandria, (c. 195, E). | • Gaius "Caligula" Caesar is born. |

# The Triumphs of the Twelve

| Year | Jewish /Idumaean History | Roman History |
|---|---|---|
| A.D. 17 / A.M. 3777 | • *"We should not gnaw and consume the soul by idleness, nor by being vexed because things happen against our wishes"* (Clement of Alexandria, c. 195, E). | • Cappadocia becomes a province.<br>• Death of Ovid, historian.<br>• Death of Livy, historian.<br>• Germanicus in the Near East (A.D. 17–18). |
| A.D. 18 / A.M. 3778 | • Caiaphas becomes high priest in Jerusalem. | • *"Among the Romans, he that commits a small theft is whipped and sent about his business"* (Bardesanes, c. 222, E). |
| A.D. 19 / A.M. 3779 | • Tiberius deports 4,000 Jews from Italy. | • Death of Germanicus, historian. |
| A.D. 20 / A.M. 3780 | • Herod Antipus builds Tiberius on the Sea of Galilee.<br>• Death of Hillel the Elder. | • Piso is prosecuted for fomenting revolt in Syria. |
| A.D. 21 / A.M. 3781 | • *From the Mishna: Slaves are forbidden to address the family head by the title of "Abba" (Father).* | • Revolt of Treveri and Aedui in Gaul.<br>• Revolt in Africa.<br>• Pens and metal writing tools appear in Rome. |
| A.D. 22 / A.M. 3782 | • *"There is another order of the Essenes who use the same customs . . .but make an alteration from these others in one respect; marriage. . . however, they make a trial of their betrothed women for a period of 3 years. . .the women likewise undergo washings in a similar manner and are also arrayed in linen garments"* (Hippolytus, c. 225, W). | • *"While in the city of an enemy captured, while still in the fury of victory, the Romans venerate the conquered deities. They seek for the Gods of strangers to make them their own. They build altars even to unknown divinities. For that reason, they have deserved their dominion. For they acknowledge the sacred institutions of all nations"* (Mark Minucius Felix, c. 200, W). |
| A.D. 23 / A.M. 3783 | • Valerius Gratis removes Annas as high priest and appoints Ishmael. | • Drusus, son of Tiberius, is murdered. |

| ɎẸear | 𝕵ewish /𝕴dumaean 𝕳istory | 𝕽oman 𝕳istory |
|-------|--------------------------|---------------|
| A.D. 24 / A.M. 3784 | • Eleazar, son of Annas, is made high priest instead of Ishmael. | • End of the revolt in Africa.<br>• Rule of Sejanus ( A.D. 23–31). |
| A.D. 25 / A.M. 3785 | • Simon, son of Camith, is made high priest in place of Eleazar. | • Sejanus unsuccessfully attempts to marry Drusus' widow. |
| A.D. 26 / A.M. 3786 | • Joseph Caiaphas, son of Innas, is made high priest instead of Simon.<br>• Baptism of John.<br>• Pontius Pilate becomes procurator of Judea. | • *Vestal Virgins perform sacrificial rites to Earth Mother Bona Dea, which are attended only by women.* |
| A.D. 27 / A.M. 3787 | • **Baptism of Jesus**<br>• **Jesus begins his public ministry.**<br>• Herod Antipas divorces his wife and marries his niece Herodias.<br>• John the Baptist denounces Herod's incestuous marriage with Herodias.<br>• **Jesus calls Philip, the first of His Twelve Apostles.** | • Tiberius leaves Rome for Capri (Capraea).<br>• Fire in Rome.<br>• Stadium in Fidenae collapses, killing 20,000.<br>• Sejanus, who dominates Tiberius, sees that Agrippina, widow of Germanicus, opposes him. |
| A.D. 28 / A.M. 3788 | • **Jesus chooses His Twelve Apostles.** | • Sejanus plots against Agrippina and her three sons and three daughters: Agrippina II, Drusilla, and Julia Livilla. |
| A.D. 29 / A.M. 3789 | • Sermon of the Feast of the Tabernacles (John 7:14–39).<br>• Raising of Lazarus from the dead.<br>• *"Christ's enemies imagined they would put Him to death, and that He, like some common mortal, would remain in Hades" (Justin Martyr, c. 160, E).* | • Agrippina, widow, is arrested and exiled with son, Nero, and three of her daughters; two sons remain free.<br>• Death of Livia, mother of Tiberius.<br>• Romans capture Sophia. |

| 𝔜ear | 𝔍ewish /𝔍dumaean 𝔥istory | 𝔎oman 𝔥istory |
|---|---|---|
| A.D. 30 / A.M. 3790 | • **Beheading of John the Baptist.**<br>• Sermon on the Mount.<br>• Triumphal entry of Jesus into Jerusalem.<br>• **Suicide of Judas Iscariot.**<br>• **Crucifixion and Resurrection of our Lord.**<br>• First Council of Christians at Jerusalem; Day of Pentecost.<br>• Apostles receive the Holy Ghost.<br>• **First Church established in Jerusalem with James the Just as head of the Church.** | • Egypt becomes a Roman province.<br>• Tournai (Belgium) is founded.<br>• Birth of Clement of Rome (d. A.D. 97).<br>• Agrippina, to protect her family, continues to oppose the growing power of Sejanus.<br>• Fl. Celsus, encyclopedia writer.<br>• *Wives convicted of adultery are banished to a small island.* |
| A.D. 31 / A.M. 3791 | • Deaths of Ananias and Sapphira for lying about their offerings.<br>• Martyrdom of Stephen.<br>• James (brother of the Lord) attacked and wounded by Saul of Tarsus. | • Murder of Nero, son of Agrippina and Germanicus.<br>• Agrippina's second son, Drusus II, is imprisoned until he dies in A.D. 33.<br>• Sejanus is executed, after his plots against Agrippina are exposed to Tiberius by his sister-in-law, Antonia. |
| A.D. 32 / A.M. 3792 | • **The Apostles call seven deacons.** | • Agrippina's third son, Gaius, who grows up to be the Emperor Caligula, is imprisoned. |
| A.D. 33 / A.M. 3793 | • Christianity begins to spread within Jerusalem.<br>• Peter meets Magi and baptizes them. | • Currency shortage in Rome. Many wealthy families are ruined.<br>• Caligula goes to Capri to join Tiberius. |
| A.D. 34 / A.M. 3794 | • Death of Herod Philip. | • *"When a rose dies, the thorn is left behind."* Ovid, Ars Amatoria. |

# Chronology

| Year | Jewish /Idumaean History | Roman History |
|------|--------------------------|---------------|
| A.D. 35 / A.M. 3795 | • Saul of Tarsus is converted to Christianity and takes the name Paul.<br>• **Matthew's Gospel written.**<br>• Birth of Ignatius (died between A.D. 98–117). | • Tiberius makes Caligula heir of his private estate.<br>• Tiberius, still suspicious of Agrippina, keeps her family in exile. |
| A.D. 36 / A.M. 3796 | • Pontius Pilate deposed, exiled.<br>• Herod Antipas remarries.<br>• Marcellus becomes governor of Judea and Syria. | • Agrippina dies while on a hunger strike.<br>• Her three daughters remain in exile. |
| A.D. 37 / A.M. 3797 | • Possible suicide of Pontius Pilate.<br>• Paul makes his first visit to Jerusalem as a Christian.<br>• Birth of Josephus (d. A.D. 96). | • Death of Tiberius.<br>• Caligula becomes emperor. He releases his three sisters from exile. He rules four years.<br>• Birth of Nero.<br>• Earthquake in Antioch. |
| A.D. 38 / A.M. 3798 | • Caligula makes Herod Agrippa King of Galilee.<br>• Anti-Jewish riots in Alexandria. | • Caligula forces his sister Drusilla to live with him as his wife. He becomes unbalanced after her suspicious death. |
| A.D. 39 / A.M. 3799 | • Caligula attempts to set up his statue in the temple at Jerusalem.<br>• Herod Antipas is deposed on a charge of treason.<br>• Philo leads delegation to Rome to protest anti-Jewish conditions in Alexandria. | • Tigellinus is banished for adultery with Caligula's sisters.<br>• Caligula puts down a conspiracy led by Gaetulicus, governor of higher Germany.<br>• Caligula banishes his sister Agrippina II and sends her son Nero, to his aunt to be raised. |
| A.D. 40 / A.M. 3800 | • Conversion of Cornelius.<br>• A Christian Church is founded in Alexandria.<br>• Early Christian Church at Corinth.<br>• Easter observance begins. | • Caligula attempts to conquer Britain, and fails miserably.<br>• Caligula makes his horse a senator.<br>• His spending has exhausted treasury surplus. |

| 𝔜ear | 𝔍ewish /𝔍dumaean 𝔥istory | 𝔯oman 𝔥istory |
|------|---------------------------|---------------|
| A.D. 41 / A.M. 3801 | • Agrippa is made king of Judea by Claudius.<br>• Claudius restores religious freedom by prohibiting Jews from proselyting.<br>• The term "Christian" comes into use for the first time. | • Death of Caligula at age 50, by stabbing, on January 24 after he had declared himself a god.<br>• Claudius succeeds him as emperor, and rules until A.D. 54.<br>• Claudius brings back Caligula's two sisters, Agrippina II and Julia Livilla, from exile.<br>• Exile of Seneca (until A.D. 49). |
| A.D. 42 / A.M. 3802 | • Antioch ministry of Paul and Barnabas. | • *"A woman is always buying something." Ovid.* |
| A.D. 43 / A.M. 3803 | • Herod Agrippa builds the walls of Jerusalem. | • Romans invade Britain. Londonium (London) is established. |
| A.D. 44 / A.M. 3804 | • **Death of James the brother of John.**<br>• Death of Herod Agrippa I.<br>• Judea annexed to Rome.<br>• Cuspus Fadus is governor of Judea.<br>• **Possible date of death of Mary, and her son, Simon Zelotes.** | • Claudius returns from Britain in triumph.<br>• Mauretania becomes a Roman province.<br>• *"Idolatry. . . is the mother of all the public amusements . . . A man has no shame if he exorcises demons in the church, but then praises their delights in the public shows" (Novation c. 235, W).* |
| A.D. 45 / A.M. 3805 | • Death of Philo.<br>• Claudius expels the Jews from Rome.<br>• **John starts his travel ministerings.** | • Agrippina II marries a wealthy man, Passienus Crispus, poisons him, and inherits his estate. |
| A.D. 46 / A.M. 3806 | • **c. James writes his epistle.** | • Thrace becomes a Roman province. |

# Chronology

| Year | Jewish / Idumaean History | Roman History |
|---|---|---|
| A.D. 47 / A.M. 3807 | • Beginning of Paul's first missionary journey.<br>• Ananias becomes high priest in Jerusalem. | • Utrecht is founded.<br>• Claudius has his wife's lover put to death. His wife is then helped to commit suicide. |
| A.D. 48 / A.M. 3808 | • Claudius makes Agrippa II superintendent of the temple in Jerusalem.<br>• **c. Judas writes his "Epistle of Jude."** | • Claudius marries Agrippina II after the death of Messalina. He adopts her son Nero.<br>• Silures revolt against Romans in Britain. |
| A.D. 49 / A.M. 3809 | • **First Epistle of Peter written.**<br>• Completion of Paul's first missionary journey.<br>• **Letter to the Galatians written.**<br>• Jerusalem Council changes circumcision rules and Gentile conversion rules. | • Silanus commits suicide, when his fiancée, Octavia, is betrothed to Nero.<br>• Seneca becomes Nero's tutor. |
| A.D. 50 / A.M. 3810 | • **First and Second Thessalonians written.**<br>• Paul's second missionary journey begins. Christianity introduced in Nubia.<br>• **Jude martyred in Ardaze, Armenia.** (legend) | • Romans learn use of soap.<br>• Basilica at Porta Maggiore is built.<br>• Cologne (Germany) is founded.<br>• Hero of Alexandria invents a steam turbine. |
| A.D. 51 / A.M. 3811 | • Jews return to Jerusalem from Rome after Roman decree against them is enforced. | • Claudius makes a decree that expels Christian Jews from Rome and the Empire. |
| A.D. 52 / A.M. 3812 | • Paul lands at Corinth.<br>• Ananias is sent to Rome, accused of violence.<br>• Thomas believed to have landed in India this year. | • Lake Fucino (Italy) is drained and the land reclaimed for cultivation.<br>• *A Roman law prohibits the execution of old or crippled slaves.* |

# The Triumphs of the Twelve

| Year | Jewish /Idumaean History | Roman History |
|---|---|---|
| A.D. 53 / A.M. 3813 | • **Luke's Gospel written.**<br>• Paul travels to Greece.<br>• **Letters to Galatians written**. | • Claudius removes Agrippa II from the tetrarchy of Chalcis. |
| A.D. 54 / A.M. 3814 | • Christianity begins to spread in Judea and the Roman Empire after the death of Claudius.<br>• Violence erupts in Caesarea over the civil rights of Jews. Nero sides with pagans. | • Death of Claudius after eating poisoned mushrooms from his wife.<br>• Nero succeeds him as emperor.<br>• Nero tries to prohibit gladiatorial games. |
| A.D. 55 / A.M. 3815 | • Felix is governor of Judea.<br>• **First and Second Corinthians, Romans written.** | • Britannicus, Claudius' son, poisoned to death by Nero.<br>• Seneca dedicates De Clementia to Nero. |
| A.D. 56 / A.M. 3816 | • *"When Polycarp was visiting Rome in the time of Anicetus, he would not forgo the observance of (Easter) customs, inasmuch as these had always been observed by John, the Disciple of the Lord, and by the other Apostles"* (Irenaeus c. 180, E/W). | • *"You [Romans] have learned geometry from the Egyptians, astronomy from the Babylonians, and the methods of healing from the Thracians. The Assyrians have also taught you many things. However, for the laws that are consistent with truth and your understandings, you are indebted to the Hebrews"* (Clement of Alexandria, c. 195, E). |
| A.D. 57 / A.M. 3817 | • Completion of Paul's Third missionary journey.<br>• Arrest of Paul in Jerusalem.<br>• He is held prisoner at Caesarea. | • War between Rome and Parthia.<br>• Nero's mother encourages an economic program that better regulates corn supply and improves general welfare. |
| A.D. 58 / A.M. 3818 | • Porcius Festus, procurator. | • Armenia becomes a Roman protectorate. |

# Chronology

| Year | Jewish /Idumaean History | Roman History |
|---|---|---|
| A.D. 59 / A.M. 3819 | • Paul leaves Melita for Rome. <br> • Joseph, son of Simon, becomes high priest. | • Nero murders his mother, Agrippina II, being influenced by his mistress, Poppea. |
| A.D. 60 / A.M. 3820 | • **Ephesians, Colossians written.** <br> • Herod Agrippa II rules northeast Judea. <br> • Paul is shipwrecked at Malta. <br> • Birth of Papias (d. A.D. 135). | • In Britain, Roman troops flog Queen Boudicca of the Iceni and rape her daughters. She vows revenge. <br> • Rhoxolani are defeated by the Romans. |
| A.D. 61 / A.M. 3821 | • **Close of the history of the Acts of the Apostles.** <br> • **Philemon, Philippians, and Hebrews written.** <br> • Birth of Pliny the Younger (d. A.D. 112). | • Queen Boudicca is defeated by the Romans after slaughtering their garrisons at Colchester, St Albans, and London. She takes poison rather than surrender. <br> • Galba becomes governor of Hispania Tarraconensis. |
| A.D. 62 / A.M. 3822 | • Gessius Florus, procurator of Judea. <br> • Completion of the temple at Jerusalem. <br> • Paul released from first Roman imprisonment. <br> • **Martyrdom of James, the brother of the Lord.** <br> • **Peter ordained head of the Church.** <br> • **Paul writes First Timothy.** | • Nero divorces Octavia and marries his mistress, Poppea. <br> • Murder of Octavia on June 9 by Nero. <br> • Fire in Rome. <br> • Earthquake in Calabria (Italy). <br> • Fall of Seneca. <br> • Death of Persius. |
| A.D. 63 / A.M. 3823 | • Festus becomes procurator of Judea. <br> • (Legend) Joseph of Arimathea goes to Glastonbury on first Christian mission to Britain. | • Armenian throne returned to Tiridates. <br> • Vespasian becomes governor of Africa. |

# The Triumphs of the Twelve

| 𝔜ear | 𝔍ewish /𝔍dumaean 𝔥istory | 𝔯oman 𝔥istory |
|------|--------------------------|----------------|
| A.D. 63 / A.M. 3823 (cont.) | • Herod's temple is finally finished. | • *"…wives have a finger ring of gold…this is not for adornment. Rather, it is for sealing things that are worth keeping safe in the house" (Clement of Alexandria, c. 195, E).* |
| A.D. 64 / A.M. 3824 | • **Paul writes Titus, Second Timothy Paul.**<br>• **Matthias dies at Sebastopol.** (legend)<br>• Christians persecuted for allegedly starting fire in Rome. | • Rome burns for 6 days and 7 nights.<br>• *"If a man drive out his father by force of arms, the Falcidian and Sempronian law would bind the murderer of his father in a sack with beasts" (Tertullian, c. 197, W).* |
| A.D. 65 / A.M. 3825 | • **c. Peter writes Second letter of Peter.** | • Execution of Seneca and Lucan.<br>• Nero kicks his pregnant wife, Poppea, in the stomach and she dies from her injuries. |
| A.D. 66 / A.M. 3826 | • Beginning of Jewish war with Rome; Zealots take Jerusalem and Sicarii capture Masada. Castius Gallus attempts to put down rebellion. | • Nero crowns Tiridates, King of Armenia.<br>• Halley's Comet was visible.<br>• Death of Petronius.<br>• Death of Thrasea Paetus. |
| A.D. 67 / A.M. 3827 | • **Martyrdom of Paul.**<br>• **Martyrdom of Peter (crucified head down), preceded by his wife.**<br>• Vespasian arrives in Jerusalem to put down Jewish revolt.<br>• Josephus, Jewish historian, captured by the Romans. | • Nero orders the building of a canal through the Isthmus of Corinth.<br>• Corbulo executed.<br>• Sardenia becomes a Roman province.<br>• *"Every god depended upon the decision of the Senate for his deity" (Tertullian, c. 197, W).* |

| 𝔜ear | 𝔍ewish /𝔍dumaean 𝔥istory | 𝔕oman 𝔥istory |
|------|--------------------------|---------------|
| A.D. 68 / A.M. 3828 | • The Essenes place the Dead Sea Scrolls in caves at Qumran.<br>• Vespasian follows Essenes to Qumran. He crushes them and Jericho.<br>• **Nathanael Bartholomew flayed alive and beheaded at Albanopolis in Armenia.**<br>• **c. John Mark writes his gospel of Mark.** | • Vindex, governor of Lyons and Galba, of eastern Spain, rise up against Nero.<br>• Suicide of Nero after having been declared persona non grata by the Senate.<br>• Galba is emperor for a few months into A.D. 69, then dies in July.<br>• *"If a man defiled freeborn boys, the Cornelian law would condemn with novel severities the crime of transgressing the sexual bond"* (*Tertullian, c 200, W*). |
| A.D. 69 / A.M. 3829 | • Titus, son of Vespasian, lays siege to Jerusalem.<br>• *"From Jerusalem, twelve men went out into the world. These were uneducated and of no ability in speaking. But by the power of God, they proclaimed to every race of men that they were sent by Christ to teach the Word of God"* (*Justin Martyr, c. 160, E*). | • Vitellus becomes emperor. He goes into hiding and dies in December.<br>• Otho becomes emperor January–April, then dies.<br>• Vespasian becomes emperor and rules until A.D. 79. |
| A.D. 70 / A.M. 3830 | • Vespasian lays siege again to Jerusalem, during Passover. Entire siege occurred between March–September. Hunger so great some resorted to eating own children.<br>• Fall and destruction of Jerusalem.<br>• **September 7—the temple is destroyed. As many as 1,100,000 Jews are killed.** | • Building begins on the Colosseum in Rome.<br>• Neapolis is founded.<br>• Germany is defeated.<br>• Borders with Armenia and Parthia strengthened.<br>• Annexation of Samothrace.<br>• *"If they believe that there is nothing after death, but declare that those who die pass into insensibility, then they become our benefactors when they set us free from sufferings"* (*Justin Martyr, c. 160, E*). |

| 𝔜ear | 𝔍ewish /𝔍dumaean 𝔥istory | 𝔯oman 𝔥istory |
|------|--------------------------|---------------|
| After A.D. 70 | • **John the Beloved writes First, Second, Third John, and Revelation, possibly from Ephesus, possibly A.D. 95.**<br>• Titus gives Judea to "Herod" Agrippa II, whose sister, Berenice, has become Titus' mistress.<br>• Titus returns to Rome with Berenice. | • Vespasian takes over Syria. Later, he builds a temple of peace in Rome. He introduces "Latin Rights," giving non-Roman townspeople civil rights. He dies June 23, A.D. 79 at the age of 69.<br>• Titus is emperor only two years.<br>• Vespasian's younger son then reigns as the Emperor Domitian until A.D. 96, when he is stabbed to death. |

# BIBLIOGRAPHY

*Atlas of World History.* New Lanark, Scotland: Geddes & Grosset, 1997.

Barton, Bruce. *ScriptureKIT Book 1: Information Pages.*

Barton, Bruce. *ScriptureKIT Book 2: Cross Referencing System.*

Bercot, David W. *A Dictionary of Early Christian Beliefs.* Peabody, MA: Hendrickson, 1998.

Brownrigg, Ronald. *The Twelve Apostles.* New York: Macmillan, 1974.

*Collins Atlas of the Bible.* Ann Arbor, MI: Borders Group Inc, 2003.

"Church History of Eusebius," *The Nicene and Post-Nicene Fathers,* Vol. 1, Bk. 1, Eerdmans, 1982.

*The Chronicle of the World.* Dorling Kindersley Limited, London, 1996.

Dorotheus, Synod de Apostol, "Synopsis ad Sim Zelot."

Durant, Will. *Caesar and Christ.* New York: Simon and Schuster, 1944.

Eisenman, Robert H. *James, the Brother of Jesus: The Key to Unlocking the Secrets of Early Christianity and the Dead Sea Scrolls.* New York: Viking, 1997.

Fairbairn, Patrick. *The Teachers' and Students' Bible Encyclopedia.* Toledo, Ohio: The Browning-Dixon Co., 1902.

Fleetwood, John. *Life of Our Lord and Savior Jesus Christ [Life of Christ].* Leipsic and Dresden: A. H. Payne. London: J. Hagger.

*Great Events of Bible Times.* London: Goldstein and Ferguson, 1987.

Hadas, Moses. *Imperial Rome.* New York: Time Life Books, 1965.

Hull, Edward. *The Wall Chart of World History.* Dorset Press, 1987.

*Life and Times of Jesus the Messiah,* Book 1, Alfred Edershiem, Eerdmans Publishers.

Maw, Herbert B. *The Apostles—Who Were They?* Salt Lake City, Utah: Publisher's Press, 1983.

McBirnie, William Steuart. *The Search for the Twelve Apostles.* Wheaton, IL: Tyndale House Publishers, 1986.

Mahan, W.D. *The Archko Volume.* Archko Press, MI, 1939.

Most, Glenn W. *Doubting Thomas.* Cambridge, MA: Harvard University Press, 2005.

Mueller, Francis John. *Christ's Twelve.* Milwaukee: Bruce Pub. Co., 1931.

The Nag Hammadi Library, James M. Robinson, Harper and Row.

*The National Comprehensive Family Bible.* London, UK, 1880.

*New Testament Apocrypha,* Vol. II, Hennecke Schneemelcher, Westminster Press.

Paffenroth, Kim. *Judas: Images of the Lost Disciple.* Louisville, KY: Westminster John Knox Press, 2001.

*Roget's International Thesaurus, Third Edition.* New York: Thomas Y. Crowell Company, 1962.

Schafer, Edward. *Ancient China.* New York : Time-Life Books, 1967.

# Bibliography

Schulberg, Lucille. *Historic India.* Alexandria, VA: Time-Life Books, 1968.

*The "Standard" Edition of The Holy Bible: Containing the King James and the Revised Versions of the Old and New Testaments Arranged in Parallel Columns [Parallel Bible of 1884].* Dayton, OH: United Brethren Publishing House, 1884.

Strode-Jackson, Myrtle. *Lives and Legends of Apostles and Evangelists.* London: Religious Tract Society, 1928.

*Strong's Concise Concordance and Vine's Concise Dictionary of the Bible.* Nashville: Thomas Nelson, 1999.

Talmage, James E. *Jesus the Christ.* Salt Lake City, UT: Deseret Book, 1970.

Trager, James. *The Women's Chronology.* Henry Holt & Co., 1994.

*Webster's Biographical Dictionary,* Springfield, Mass.: G. & C. Merriam Co., 1969.

*Webster's Encyclopedia Unabridged Dictionary of the English Language.* New York: Portland House, 1989.

Accept me,
  O Christ Jesus.
Whom I saw,
Whom I love,
  and in
Whom I am.

Accept my spirit
  in peace
  in Your Eternal Realm.

Last prayer of Andrew the
Apostle, tied to his 𝕏.